A PROPHET
FOR
THE PRIESTHOOD

by
John A. Hardon, S.J.

Imprimatur: † René H. Gracida
Bishop of Corpus Christi
March 19, 1997

Published and Distributed with the Permission of Inter Mirifica Inc. by:

Eternal Life, Bardstown, KY 40004-0787

Commendation

There seem to be no end to the jewels that flow from the mind, heart and pen of Father Hardon. Father Gerald C. Fitzgerald's life comes alive thanks to his many talents.

Father Gerald offers much good advice, compassionate and compelling. Every priest should read it.

In the hands of good Catholic laity it will doubtless be both efficacious and persuasive in arousing their prayer on behalf of priests and in building a greater zeal to promote vocations.

CONTENTS

Fr. John A. Hardon, S.J.
1914-2000

"Unless we recover the zeal and the spirit of the first century Christians — unless we are willing to do what they did and to pay the price that they paid, the future of our country, the days of America are numbered."

Prayer for the Glorification of Fr. John A. Hardon, S.J.

We thank you, O Lord! for having blessed your Church with the untiring service of your priest, John Hardon.

May he, from heaven, continue his mission and obtain for us the strength and the intelligence to proclaim and defend the truth with genuine fidelity to the Catholic Faith and the charity he drew from the Sacred Heart of Jesus.

Grant us, we pray, the favors we ask through his intercession and raise him to the honors of the altar. Amen.

His Eminence
Edouard Cardinal Gagnon, p.s.s.

Eternal Life
Bardstown, KY 40004-0787
1-800-842-2871
orders@lifeeternal.org

PREFACE

As a member of the Congregation of Holy Cross, it is indeed a distinct pleasure for me to have been asked to preface a book that is entitled a spiritual biography of Father Gerald M.C. Fitzgerald, a former member of my Institute and the founder of two distinct religious Institutes, the *Servants of the Paraclete* and the *Handmaids of the Precious Blood.*

Father Fitzgerald left the Congregation of Holy Cross only because of a Divine touch of the Holy Spirit that had inspired in his priestly heart the seed of a specific and new charism in the life of the Church, a seed which was planted, when as a diocesan priest of Boston before joining the Congregation of Holy Cross, he opened the door of a rectory in Brighton, Massachusetts where he was serving, only to find before him an "off-duty priest" who was "out of work" and begging for food and help. (Golden Jubilee, Handmaids of the Precious Blood, 1997, p.4)

As has been true down through human history, Divine Providence has always known exactly when and how to meet the challenges which His Bride the Church has to face in carrying out the sublime task which He has given her, by choosing certain persons, whom He has selected from all eternity, to play a specific and precise role in that Divine Symphony, which is the continuous "playing out" of that universal "Song of Songs" that we call "salvation history". And so it was in the case of Father Gerald M.C. Fitzgerald.

During his years as a chaplain in the United States Army during World War II, the seed which had been planted that night at the rectory in Brighton, began to unfold. During the conflict, Father Fitzgerald strongly felt an inspiration of our Lord and His Mother, to bring forth two religious Institutes, distinct but complementary in

i

their scope, which centered on the priesthood. One was a community of men, priests and brothers, who would dedicate their lives to giving direct care to priests in need, both material and spiritual. The other was a community of religious women, who would live a simple contemplative prayer-life, offering their hidden sacrifices and sufferings for the sanctification of souls and the holiness of God's priests. And thus the idea of the "Servants of the Paraclete" and the "Handmaids of the Precious Blood" was born (Ibid., p.3).

As the reader goes through this life story of Father Gerald Fitzgerald, the founder of the *Servants* and *Handmaids*, whose priestly mind has been so well illuminated and "filmed" in this spiritual biography, he or she will find a man who was chosen by Divine Providence to teach priests who they are and for what purpose they have been chosen, ordained and sent forth. As Father John Hardon, S.J., the author of this biography remarks: "A priest is a man of faith who is ordained to sustain and nourish the faith of others today as at the very beginning of the Church" (A Prophet for the Priesthood, A Spiritual Biography of Father Gerald Fitzgerald, s.P., pp. 4-5). Father Gerald saw in the service and functions of the priest, not a human creation, but rather a creation of the Holy Spirit in and through the workings of the Trinity. It is, therefore, not at all to be wondered at that the founder whose life is presented in this spiritual biography, named his Congregation of religious priests and brothers *Servants of the Paraclete*, and chose Pentecost as the feast on which his Congregation of religious women, the *Handmaids of the Precious Blood*, was to be established. These two Institutes were founded to sacrifice the lives of their members for priests: those who have been faithful, so that they might remain always loyal to Christ their Master; and those who have strayed, so that they might return to the one who ordained them for His service (cf. Fr. Hardon, op. Cit., p. 5).

It will become ever more evident in the course of the book that Father Gerald was a man consumed by the "Gift and Mystery" of the priesthood, not unlike the leader of the universal Church today, Pope John Paul II. And it was this charism, which is a gift of the same Holy Spirit, that he bequeathed to his two Institutes. As he himself remarked on the occasion of the foundation of the *Handmaids*: "The Servants of the Paraclete are to work directly with and for priests; and the Handmaids, in their contemplative life of perpetual adoration, are to pray and sacrifice for the sanctification of all priests, especially those in spiritual need, and for the needs of all people throughout the world" (cf. <u>Golden Jubilee</u>, etc. p.6). What we have in the foundation of the two Institutes is a perfect complementarity of action on the part of two <u>distinct</u> Institutes, which while using different means, have one ultimate scope: the good of the priesthood. As Father Gerald was accustomed to repeat on various occasions: "The priesthood is God's greatest gift to man. Its faithful fulfillment is man's greatest gift to God" (cf. Fr. Hardon, p.5).

He saw that the greatest mistake of priests who fail God in their fidelity to the promises of their ordination was to forget that ordained priests, like their Master, the first High Priest, must also be victims. To make up for this mistake, he intended that the life of the *Servants* and even more visibly so, because of the contemplative "call", that of the *Handmaids*, must attempt to remain "lifted up", as a way of drawing all things to Him, so that all priests would remain faithful to that fundamental part of their "call" which is to "hold Him and not let Him go" (<u>Song of Songs</u>, 3:4).

As the reader meditates on the contents of this spiritual biography, it is the hope of the undersigned priest that he or she will be able to capture and assimilate the profound love which this priest-founder, whose spiritual odyssey is revealed throughout, had for the "Gift and Mystery" of the priesthood, which he was convinced was God's greatest gift to the Church and to all human beings. It is my hope that this recognition will become a conviction and that the reflective reading of this book will assist such readers, to pray and sacrifice for this "Gift and Mystery", and for those who are called by God's personal act of love for His Church and for them, to incarnate it.

Rome, August 6, 1997 † Charles A. Schleck, C.S.C.
Feast of the Transfiguration Titular Archbishop of Africa
Adjunct Secretary
Congregation for the
Evangelization of Peoples

INTRODUCTION

The Catholic Church is a permanent miracle of God's providence. From the days of her Founder she has been oppressed and persecuted, opposed and betrayed. Yet she stands after nineteen centuries stronger than ever and rising above her enemies as the City of God on earth. Already in the second century, Tertullian made the observation that has since become a motto, "The blood of martyrs is the seed of the Church." The Church actually thrives on her sufferings. No less than her Founder she continues to redeem the world by the shedding of her blood.

However, it is not trial and suffering alone that has so abundantly provided for the Church's supernatural prosperity over the centuries. The trials and problems of the Church had to be met by outstanding leaders whom the Spirit of Christ raised in times of crisis, to staunch the blood and heal the wounds of the Mystical Body. With rare exception, these leaders were men and women who became founders of religious institutes that carried on the spirit of those who established them, and thus insured that what was originally begun would continue, even for centuries, after the founder had entered eternity.

After the Church had been liberated under Constantine in the early fourth century, men like Antony of Egypt and Pachomius arose to prepare the Church interiorly through the creation of monastic communities in the Mediterranean world. Two centuries later when the Church began her work of civilizing western Europe, St. Benedict became the father of generations of religious who were to evangelize the barbarians of that day. With the rise of industrialism in the early thirteenth century and the threat to Christianity from the use of money as a means of profit, Francis of Assisi appeared on the scene. He preached a return to the Gospels and a return to the poverty of Christ that preserved the Church from going the way of all flesh, when money becomes the guiding motive in people's lives. In the same century, the intellectual world began to challenge the simple truths of the Christian faith, so Dominic was inspired to found the Order of Preachers who became the Church's teachers to preserve the faith among the rising intelligentsia of the early Renaissance. In the sixteenth century, when the unity of Christendom was broken by the Protestant reformers, the Lord chose Ignatius of Loyola to defend the foundations of this unity, centered in the papacy. He added to the three customary vows of poverty, chastity and obedience, a special vow of allegiance to the Vicar of Christ for his professed members. In the seventeenth century when the growing wealth of the people made them forget the needs of their neighbor, Vincent de Paul became the apostle of charity to remind the faithful that sharing what they had with the poor was the condition of their own salvation. St. Louise de Marillac, spiritual daughter of Vincent, became the mother of innumerable families of consecrated women who, as angels of mercy, prove that Christ is still on earth to care for the sick and the halt and the lame and the blind, and to care for children who are specially beloved by the Master.

So the litany of God's Providence has gone on. Always a new crisis brought into existence a new leader. Problems facing the Church became challenges to be met by persons who, not unlike the prophets of old, saw themselves as messengers of Yahweh to teach the people His truth and to lead them in His ways.

No one familiar with the present age has any doubt that the Church has been going through a grave crisis for over a century. Some consider it the gravest in the Church's history and certainly its impact on the Church and her institutions has been drastic in the extreme. Under the general name of secularism it is the philosophy which claims that there is no other life than "this life" and no other world than "this world." If there is an after life, and the secularist is ready to grant the possibility, it is so uncertain and improbable that the hypothesis has no practical value in determining a person's behavior. By now there is a variety of secularisms in the world. But they all have this in common: they hold the meaning of the world to lie within itself.

It would be unrealistic to expect the Church to remain unaffected by present day secularism. Catholics are too much a part of the culture in which they live and too exposed to the ideas of their day not to be influenced by what they experience. Add to this secularism the rise of the communications media in the twentieth century and we get some idea of how inevitably the Church has suffered by contact with the unbelieving world in which she lives.

Among the Church's institutions the priesthood has been especially vulnerable. This may be partly explained by the fact that priests are the Church's divinely established leaders of faith and morals, but mainly by the strategy of the evil spirit who could be expected to intrude himself into the ranks of Christ's chosen ones. For even as the Church's greatest pride is in the sanctity of her ordained bishops and priests who lead the people of God in the paths of holiness, so they have been the Church's greatest sorrow when they abandoned their high calling and turned their backs on the Savior who ordained them.

The modern Popes have been eloquent in stressing the grave need of a strong priesthood to resist the pressure against the faith in our times. Leo XIII and Pius X, Benedict XV and Pius XI, Pius XII and John XXIII have pleaded time and again with bishops and priests to resist the seductions of a godless world and remain firm in their loyalty to Christ and His Church. No one could be clearer than Paul VI when, on the occasion of ordaining ten priests to the Episcopate, he urged them to remain constant in their faith. "It is the gift of Christ to His Church," he said. "It is the virtue that the Church needs today, assailed as she is by so many forces that aim at defeating her, indeed weakening and destroying her firmness in faith." It is faith, he told the newly ordained prelates, "that must protect us from our inner weakness and against the growing confusion of ideas of our world."[1]

In the first year of his pontificate, Pope John Paul II wrote to the priests of the Catholic world, urging them to resist the temptation to compromise with the world. "What the people expect of their ordained leaders," he said, "is above all a priestly personality that witnesses to a world beyond this one and to values that belong to eternity. Priests should not be deceived. Sometimes the people may want priests to be in every way like them'; at times it even seems that they demand this of us." A priest must be on his guard. "It is very easy to let oneself be guided by appearances and fall victim to a fundamental illusion in what is essential. Those who call for the secularization of priestly life and applaud its various manifestations will surely abandon us if we give in to the temptation. We shall then cease to be necessary and popular." The Pope went on to explain how careful priests must be to avoid being manipulated and exploited by a world that wants to shape everyone, especially the Church's leaders, to its own image and likeness.[2]

The subject of our spiritual biography, Father Gerald Fitzgerald, clearly understood this teaching of the Bishops of Rome. He knew, as few of his contemporaries did, that what the Church in modern times most needs is priests who have not been seduced by the ways of the world but have remained firm in their faith as ambassadors of Christ, chosen by Him to dispense the mysteries of salvation until the end of time.

As we go through the life story of Father Gerald and look into his priestly mind, we shall find a man who was chosen by Providence to teach priests who they are and why they were ordained. In his own words, "A good priest is a prisoner of love for Our Lord because Our Lord is a prisoner of love for him." A priest, therefore, is a man of faith who is ordained to sustain and nourish the faith of others, just as much in the twentieth century as in the first. It is the same Christ now through the power of priestly consecration as lived on earth then.

Father Gerald appreciated the excellence of this free gift of God to man and would quote St. John Chrysostom, whose exalted view of the priesthood appealed to his own poetic spirit: "Although the priesthood is exercised on earth it rightfully belongs to the celestial realm. For it was no man, nor angel, nor archangel, nor any other created power that arranged this function, but the Holy Spirit Himself, and it was He, too, that inspired men to seek the ministry of angels." Thus, it was not surprising to find him naming his congregation of priests and brothers Servants of the Paraclete, and choosing Pentecost, of set purpose, as the feast on which his congregation of Sisters, the

Handmaids of the Precious Blood, were founded. His thoughts often returned to the gratuitous favor of God to His unworthy servants in a phrase which became something of a motto: "The priesthood is God's greatest gift to man. Its faithful fulfillment is man's greatest gift to God."

I. MODERN SECULARISM AND THE PRIESTHOOD

There is a basic problem that the founder of the Paracletes and Handmaids raises for anyone who is concerned, as he was, with the status of the Catholic priesthood in the modern world. The problem is, "Whatever happened to the priesthood?" Why has the Church, at least in the Western world, been plagued with so many, thousands in a few years, defections from the priestly ministry? Why have vocations to the priesthood in some countries dropped to an all-time low? Why have so many priests made public spectacles of themselves, through the press and media, in criticizing, if not ridiculing, the papacy, celibacy and the Church's unmistakable moral teaching?

Many explanations can be given, and by now scores have been made, to try to account for the crisis of the priesthood that no one, except those who are part of it, will deny. But there is one explanation that deserves our special attention, because given by the subject of the present study. Father Gerald would say there is a crisis in the priesthood because there is a crisis in modern society. The secularism of our day has affected the Church and infected her priests; or, better, there is a problem in the Catholic priesthood wherever and to the extent that secular philosophy has penetrated the ranks of Christ's ordained.

In less sophisticated language, the underlying difficulty that has created so many problems is the rise of a new idolatry. It is the idolatry of self, more commonly known as pride. Although as old as humanity, it has taken on a new capacity for making converts, partly because of the newly discovered means of social communication and partly because the evil spirit seems to be more than ever active in seducing souls to his cause.

Speaking of his own life-time experience with priests and specifically of those for whom he labored in the apostolate, Father Gerald said, "It would be my honest conclusion that eighty-five percent, perhaps even more, ninety-five percent of the problems that bring priests to Via Coeli have their root in pride. A proud man will not stop following his course of folly; a humble man will learn even by his mistakes. A proud man will not learn; he refuses to learn even by his mistakes. A humble man, if he offends God, no matter in what virtue it may be, will come back to his God and say: I'm sorry. The proud man cannot say: I'm sorry. Because pride is self-deification. One makes oneself one's god and says even to God: *Non serviam*, I will not serve."[1]

AFFLUENCE AND ATHEISM

There is some value in exploring this phenomenon of modern pride if we are to make sense of what has happened in the priesthood and to be able to reform what needs reformation.

A large contributing factor that has stimulated man's occupation with himself and forgetfulness of God is the rise, certainly in America, of an extraordinary access to the good things of this world. "We have a boasted affluent society." Americans are told, "We never had it so good." Look at us! "We crowd the golf courses today. We are cruising in powerboats and sailboats and yachts over the bays, and the lakes and the oceans that surround us. We are bathing in the balmy weather wherever American industry will carry us on commercial tours. We have a forty-hour week. We have cars and every material convenience."[2] All of this is common knowledge and, in varying degrees, available to millions.

Yet all the while that people are becoming immersed in these naturally satisfying experiences, they are becoming less interested in God and the things of the spirit.

We have within us a built-in intelligence which allows us to dominate the whole kingdom which graces the whole visible universe at our feet and gives us the universe to conquer. And God invites us to conquer it. But the problem among the children of men is not the conquering of this visible universe — we haven't begun to conquer ourselves. That's the problem.

Man can land on the moon, but so what! There is every indication that a human being on the moon can be as unhappy as we are by the millions down here on earth. And if you land a second man there is no reason why the two of them might not have a fight to death over it. Man has made tremendous, appalling, startling progress in the physical and material sciences, but oh how woefully he has failed in the science that is most important of all to human happiness and even happiness essential for human co-existence, social relations of the national and international basis.[3]

Along with affluence has developed a callous indifference to the needs of others. We boast of our prosperity, "in the face of the fact that millions of our fellow beings even in this country are hungry tonight." We indulge in pleasures of the flesh — and satisfy our emotions while so many of our people are desperately looking for meaning in life. They are "in agonizing defeat that leads them at last to revolt." What is wrong?

Man has failed in the most important of all relations, his relations with God and with his fellow man. Never before has atheism raised its ugly head so blatantly and openly, inviting the lightning of God's disaster, God's retribution. Unless men believe, they cannot please God, and unless men believe in Jesus Christ, even if they have perfect human relations within the nation and internationally, what do they have? If all man's powers or glory and happiness led only to the grave, O Jesus, what would we have? The more that life was filled with happiness, if the grave ended it all, the greater the tragedy. The happier a man or woman was, the sadder would be the hour of their leaving.[4]

These are the conclusions of a believer as he looked at the results of what man's genius produces when it seeks only his own personal and collective gratification separated from God.

The first factor, then, that helps explain the modern crisis in the priesthood is the conflict between worldly prosperity and the "narrow way" of Christ that leads to salvation. When the Master said those are few who walk His way, because the ways of the world are more naturally appealing, He included some of His anointed ones, who would choose mammon to God and even defend their choice as more relevant or contemporary or "in touch with the times."

Only deep humility, born of faith, is a match for the subtle worldliness that surrounds priests today like the atmosphere they breathe. Hence the need for prayer, asking the Savior what the disciples asked from Him in Palestine: "O Lord Jesus, increase our faith. And thank You for our faith. I believe in one God. I believe in a Father who created me. I believe in a Son who came out of the happiness of His Father's bosom in order to share my life and to invite me to share His life as victim, host and priest."[5]

Nothing but this kind of faith will sustain a priest in today's climate of selfish affluence.

NEED OF PRAYER

It is almost to be expected that pride leads to a neglect of prayer. After all, whatever else prayer is, it is the acknowledgment of God's greatness and my littleness: His goodness and readiness to give and my terrible and constant need of His help. But proud people do not pray, in the exact measure of their pride. Only humble people are honest enough to admit that God alone is God and they are simply they.

In light of this truth of faith and fact of human experience it is revealing to be told that, where priests have difficulties, there is a universal explanation.

> The greatest problem we have in the lives of the priests is neglect of prayer. They tell me that they forget — they were so busy building churches, running bazaars, taking care of clubs that little by little prayer went out of their lives. How does this apply in our lives? If you are going to be successful in the spiritual life, you must fall in love with the business of prayer. Prayer must be, not a burden, but a joy.[6]

Therein lies the hub of the problem; for so many priests prayer has become a burden and so they relieve themselves of the weight as often and for as long as they can.

What Father Gerald says about "building churches" and "taking care of clubs" is only symptomatic of a wider issue that affects every priest, and bishop, no matter what his activity may be. There is no apostolic work in which a priest engages that cannot become for him an excuse for praying less than he should, or even giving up prayer altogether. But always, no matter what the reason, it is an excuse. Why? Because for a man who really understands his priesthood and wants to live it as he should, there can be no legitimate grounds for neglecting prayer, because there is no one under God who needs to pray more than a priest.

<u>Adoration</u>. Why must everyone, and, therefore with emphasis, why must priests pray? The fundamental reason is that our primary obligation is to worship God. "Your primal purpose as rational creatures and as priests of God. . . is to adore your God and keep Him loving company. That's your first duty and nothing takes its place."[7]

Not only is prayer the primary duty of a priest, it is also his greatest privilege.

> What a privilege to adore one's God. The ultimate and highest activity of a rational creature is to adore with grateful love, appreciation, understanding, oblation, the Supreme Being who has given him existence; who has given him more than existence, strange as that may seem, by redemption; and who is intent on perfecting the image of the beauty of God in the individual soul, which is the result of sanctification.

> Dear Fathers, never forget the element of adoration. The more you adore God, the more God will draw you to Himself, and that which seems so attractive in creation will find its absorption in the divine goodness and loveliness and beauty of God.[8]

On both counts, therefore, as a duty and privilege, a priest should pray and witness to others that he prays, because he has been ordained to testify to the world that there is an infinite God who deserves and demands His creatures' recognition and the evidence of their submission to His Divine Majesty.

We are above all other creatures called upon to adore God — we are the formal, official representatives of God, and the basic attitude of a creature to its God is adoration: *Venite adoremus*, come let us adore Him. We have come with gifts from the East to adore Him, to offer Him adoration: that immolation of the human spirit in the presence of Divinity. Now since we are always in the presence of Divinity, the ideal of the contemplative soul — and you must aim at being contemplative souls according to the degree of grace that God will give you. Our Lord Himself is the model: from the first moment of His existence in His Mother's bosom, His whole Heart, His whole Being was in adoration, so the humanity of Our Lord was absorbed in adoration of the Divinity.

So for a faithful priest it becomes a deep instinct, a habitual attitude of the soul. The soul rests in the presence of God like a little child whose eyes follow its mother wherever the mother goes; the little child remains in loving contemplation of its mother. So in the depths of your souls — it works this way — the more you cultivate this interior union with God which adoration brings about, the more you will find contentment and happiness. You will be able to deal with the unreasonableness and cruelties of man, including the cruelties of God's priests to God, that we must bear with.[9]

But how is a busy priest, involved in so many things, to keep up this practice of adoring prayer? One method is "by the use of a repeated phrase, to stir the soul and to renew the soul, like the little ticking of a clock. The soul can say to God habitually, *Adoro Te, adoro Te, adoro Te*. Fill in the little breaks in the mortar of activity with the cement of a momentary elevation of the soul to the Trinity, any phrase by which you lift yourself to the Adorable Trinity."[10]

If the natural, worldly attitude is to become so preoccupied with creatures as to forget about the Creator, the supernatural habit that a priest must cultivate is just the opposite, namely the practice of constant prayer.

Immolation. There is a special kind of adoration which is very pleasing to God, and that priests are literally ordained to practice. This is the prayer of sacrifice, or what Father Gerald calls immolation.

It is noteworthy that the one time when Christ specially urged His disciples to pray was when He was in the Garden of Gethsemane. And the one time when He gave us the most eloquent example of how to pray was during His agony. What is most significant is the fact that Christ did not actually have to pray, as though, being God, He needed the help that without prayer He would not have received. His prayer was an act of adoration, but the adoration of sacrifice. And His urging the apostles on that occasion to pray was not only, or mainly, to obtain the strength they (unlike Him) certainly needed "not to be put to the test" (Luke 22:40); it was principally that, in prayer, they would acknowledge God's sovereignty and show they were submitting to His Divinity.

> Is this the doctrine of Christ? It certainly is the doctrine of Christ. Our Lord said on one occasion that we should pray always. He Himself, being in the Agony, gave Himself to further prayer. And our prayer can be an immolation especially when the soul is in great suffering, in desolation. It can place itself, humble itself in adoration to the Divine Will and when the soul does that, then God must always smile upon it. Actually God is always with the soul even if the soul is not aware of it. Live a life of adoration and if you do that you will find yourself without frustration at the end of the day and at the end of life.

> Adoration then is the *A*, the Alpha of priestly existence. Now God has given us His own life to adore but God Himself does not adore. What does He do? God blesses.[11]

That closing sentence is very meaningful. Those who adore God are blessed by God. They give Him what, as God, He demands but does not need. He gives them what they need but have no right to demand. More than once in the Scriptures, we are told that God blesses those who bless Him. Those who worship the Almighty open the doors to omnipotence; they tap resources of divine power that no one else can expect to achieve.

And this access to God's blessings, as the reward for giving God His due, is especially fruitful when the adoration is costly, that is, when it is immolation. This, in fact, is the real meaning of a priestly priesthood: when the one who offers the sacrifice of the Mass unites his sacrifices with that of Christ, and in doing so becomes a more effective channel of salvation to a sinful mankind.

UNION WITH GOD

Father Gerald never tired of urging his followers to help priests respect their high calling and not be so involved in other activity as to become ineffective in working for souls. "God didn't ordain us for these other activities. He didn't need to ordain us for them." Why then? "We were ordained to link men to God, and to do that we must be linked ourselves to God."[12]

Failure here has serious consequences. Admittedly, "there is always danger of an over simplification. But would it not seem a reasonable comment on the priesthood of America today to say that we are not successfully, efficiently, as far as numbers are concerned, linking people to God because we are not closely linked to God ourselves?"[13]

This is not so much an indictment as the sober conclusion from observable facts. Where and when and in the degree that priests are truly men of God, they win souls from Satan and for Christ out of all proportion to their numbers or natural abilities. Who were "the greatest of God's disciples of the active apostolate" among priests? They "have all been men who have been 'hidden in Christ.' St. Francis Xavier spent long hours in prayer with Our Lord, as did Ignatius, John Baptist Vianney. You cannot find a saint who was not, and is not, 'hidden in Christ.'"[14] Without exception, God uses those who are most closely united with Him to accomplish His greatest work for souls.

Why should this be so? The final reason is a mystery, but one reason is undoubtedly that, just as in nature like reproduces like, so in the order of grace holy people reproduce themselves in sanctifying others. And since priests are to be the principal channels of God's grace by their ministry and teaching, their union with God should be outstanding — seeing how much the faithful depend on their ministrations.

Christ is and Christ is forever! If I do not bring the people of God to Him I have done nothing. If I am not afire with His love I am like an acolyte trying to light the candles with an unlit taper. My own personal ego can only burn with a human flame, a naturalism, unless I have buried myself with Christ and am able to say with St. Paul, "I live, no not I, but Christ lives in me."

One of the deepest errors that we are witnessing in the Church of God at this time is the attempt to rush into the lives of others before we have lost ourselves in the life of Christ. I am going to lead men and women to God by walking with Christ. If I walk with Christ — if I live with Christ — then the world will come to my doorstep. This does not mean that we are indifferent to the fruitage of the cruel social, national and international injustices of the past which we are reaping in this country and which is being reaped all over the world, but it means this: I will be able to reassure and strengthen the faith and give motivation to those whose life is by the plan of God already committed to be the image of Christ in the family, in the parish, in the community, in the inner city, in the battle lines that are being drawn on our university campuses.[15]

The error to which Father Gerald refers is no minor mistake. It is, as he knew and subsequent events have borne out, somewhere near the center of what we began by calling a crisis in the priesthood. Since Father Gerald made these comments the year of his death, perhaps a hundred other explanations have been given and as many solutions offered for the loss of faith among so many faithful; the growing instability of family life among Catholics; and their increased acceptance of premarital relations, contraception, and even the abortion of unwanted children.

The founder of Via Coeli would lay these and similar aberrations, at least partially, on the consciences of priests. "Whenever a priest who loves God says Mass, the people gather around him as bees gather around a honeycomb for they know that if he is a man of God he will give them the honey of the Truths of the Gospel for their minds, the flaming fire of Divine Love to lift their weak human wills and inflame them with a love to crucify themselves. Those who are Christ's have crucified themselves."[16] But that is the key. A priest must have died to himself in his love for Christ so that others will be led to do the same because Christ uses him as a catalyst for their sanctification. Or even more emphatically, as a priest "If I am a man of God, I will draw the people of God to God."[17] Where people are not being thus transformed, this means they need more men of God to draw them to their Lord.

POOREST OF THE POOR

Mother Teresa of Calcutta has become world-famous because of her work among "the *poorest of the poor*." Her Constitutions specify that the Missionaries of Charity specialize in working among these outcasts of society, whose number is greater than most people imagine and whose condition is deplorable in the extreme. In countries like India they die in the streets, untended, unwanted and, except for the charity of some heroic souls, even unknown as they enter eternity.

Father Gerald applied this expressive name to men who were ordained to the altar and are leaving this life without appreciating their awesome dignity.

> Is there any beggar in the world so pitifully poor as the priest of God who dies not appreciating his priesthood? Dear God! The man who receives the priesthood has received the greatest gift that God can give to an individual man: His Priesthood. He is Himself in the priesthood. When He gives Himself to us in Holy Communion, He does indeed give Himself, but when He gives Himself in the priesthood He gives Himself in such a way that the priest can give Him to others — to His Father and to His people.[18]

It is to these desperately poor men that Father Gerald directed his apostolic efforts, and in their interest that he organized the Paracletes and Handmaids.

> There is no one in the world so poor as one who dies not understanding how rich he is. And so, in working for those

who are in the state of not appreciating their priesthood, we are working for those who are the poorest of the poor. We know that Jesus Christ has stamped these souls with His image, and so we know without having any visions that what we do for them we do for Christ Himself. Christ is imprisoned in their souls and we can help Him to open the door and set Him free. In setting Christ free, they set themselves free and like Lazarus they come out of the tomb into Easter morning, into the daily living of the good Christian. What a beautiful vocation, to "slash your lives" and give them to Christ in the poorest of the poor![19]

Only God knows how many such men there are.

What is sadly true is that there are enough today who are so confused about their identity, they give up their priestly ministry for the most appalling reasons. "When priests betray Our Lord it is for less than thirty pieces of silver, is it not? After all, the silver had done no evil, the silver had not enticed of its own, if the silver could have spoken, it would have said: O Judas do not take us for our Creator; we are only gleaming dust, He is gleaming Divinity. All sin is the choosing of the dust. Even when it is the choosing of a living creature, what are we but animated dust? And what is the source of our animation? All the beauty of human love, all the beauty and tenderness that is in honest human love, is only a fraction, a faint shadow of the tenderness of God's love that waits for God's priests in His Heart and in the beautiful silver chalice of His Mother's Heart."[20]

The secret, therefore, to a priest's appreciation of his true worth and the only sure protection against infidelity is the satisfaction that comes to one who, in faith, is totally dedicated to Christ. He should be able to exclaim, and mean it, "Oh, the joy of being a priest!" He should be convinced that "a priest is a link between God and souls; he is the link, Christ in him or he in Christ, whichever way you wish."[21]

But then a question arises, and it must be answered by every priest for himself if he is to recognize his worth in a world that sees in him only another man, and no different from anyone else.

There is a natural linking to our fellow creatures; our linking with God has to be supernatural. A normal man loves companionship. It's so natural to be gracious to his fellow man, to smile on the world, for a mentally well-balanced individual. But what about the link with God? That requires supernatural activity. That requires, if it is to be a deep and permanent linking, long hours of Eucharistic adoration. That requires pleading with God: "Lord, fasten me more firmly into your Sacred Heart so that nothing in the world shall take me away from it." Every priest in trouble has the basis in his will and is a priest who has been, at least partially, or temporarily, taken away from God. Taken away from God. So we should plead with Our Lord to fasten us more deeply into His Sacred Heart.[22]

This is the language of faith, that every priest should strive to learn and speak with increasing ease. In practice it means that he must spend all the time he can in the company of his Eucharistic Lord. It further means he must never cease pleading with God to convince him that "nothing the world has to offer — the sensual body, the lustful eye, pride in possessions — could ever come from the Father but only from the world; and the world, with all it craves for, is coming to an end." This kind of conviction the priest needs if he is to convince others that "only the person who does the will of God remains forever" (I John 2:16-17).

II. What Is a Priest?

It is impossible to grasp Father Gerald's great love and concern for the priesthood, unless we see something of his understanding of what a priest is. During his lifetime, he did things that others misunderstood. He traveled many thousands of miles, to distant countries, and across the United States many times, in the interest of the priesthood. He literally exhausted himself in urging bishops to support his efforts for Christ's anointed ones, and in the pursuit of his vision he allowed himself to die estranged from the Via Coeli he had spent years in creating in order to serve the poorest of Christ's poor, the priests who were in trouble and who wanted to return to the active service in the priesthood.

All his labors make sense only on the premise that a priest is something unique; in fact so unique that it required the Incarnation of the Son of God to make it possible.

Ten years before his death, in a conference he gave shortly before Christmas to the Handmaids of the Precious Blood, he opened his heart on what, to his mind, the Catholic priesthood means. Most of the present chapter will be the words of this conference. The author of these pages will step aside to allow Father Gerald to pour out his soul.

What makes the conference memorable is that it was given to religious women specially dedicated to serve Christ's priests, that it showed a keen awareness of the noble vocation to marriage and rearing a family, and that it explains why Gerald was so passionately insistent on priests being holy priests, seeing how great was their calling and how important their role in the economy of salvation.

When one speaks of the priesthood, one is looking on something that is vast like the ocean, or like a mountain range. There are many roads leading into a mountain and many harbors border on the sea, so I am going to take, as a sort of way of tying it in, a quotation that is in one of the chapels here in the Canyon; something I said some years ago. What I said was this: "The priesthood is God's greatest gift to man. Its faithful fulfillment is man's greatest gift to God."

Now, why do I make that little distinction? Because the priesthood is never seen in the abstract. Even if Christ were [visibly] here, the Great High Priest, it would not be an abstraction; it would be Christ, the High Priest.

We don't see the priesthood. It doesn't walk around except as it is specified and integrated in the souls of men. When you treat of the priesthood in the abstract, you have this sublimity, but when that sublimity is translated into the actuality of daily living, it is identified with a human being, with a man, who according to the various reactions of his soul to the Will and Providence of God, fills the part and is identified with the priesthood.

First, let us take the original half of the statement, "The priesthood is God's greatest gift to man," and consider it in the light of the Church's teaching.

There are two great basic purposes that God has revealed in creation and redemption. Now, of course, in the Divine Mind they come into the Divine unity, with the glory of God the fundamental purpose. But by our Catholicism, we believe God, as a Supreme Being, could be "fruitful". . . as the Godhead is, in the Son and in the Spirit; that is the "fruitfulness" of God within His own Divine nature.

This is a very wonderful truth and is sort of satisfying, that God is not lonely, that within the Divine nature, there is not only a Father, but a Son who loves Him, and a Spirit who is their bond of love; sort of making a perfect setup, the equivalent and the source of family life.

God realizes that He can share the gift of existence with creatures as part of His power and wisdom. So He wills to create and He dares to create a creature to His own image and likeness. He creates man to His own image and likeness and that means that man has a rational nature, even though his body is fashioned out of the clay of the earth. Because God breathes into this clay a living soul and thus you have in the image of God shadowed in the clay the reality of God, the earnestness of God. God is not setting up a tin soldier, or a little plastic figurine. God is in earnest and so you have stemming out of that the first basic vocation of life, which is a very wonderful and a very holy one, the participation in God and with God in carrying on the work of creation, by which you and I had a mother and father and received the gift of life.

So you have the married state as a vocation which is a sublime and holy thing. God has honored man with the dignity of co-creationism, with Himself, of course, in our Catholic philosophy of truth, serving as He did in fashioning the slime of the earth by created forms, yet He breathes into it the living soul. Father and mother gave us [bodily] existence, but God Himself creates the soul of man. That's the normal vocation of life to which the vast majority of men and women are called, to participate in the tremendous and holy and joyous work of creating the throb of love that was in the bosom of God from all eternity.

But there is a second and higher phase of God's revelation of divine love. Even as He was creating man, God foresaw that man would abuse his gift of freedom.

From all eternity God foresaw that man would fall into the folly of sin, which we call original sin because it goes back to the origin of the race, and brought it to pass automatically that all the children of men on earth were to stem back to disobedient parents and would have forfeited by the sin of their first parents the tremendous privilege of being conceived in the state of sanctifying grace.

Here we come to the second vocation in which you and I participate. The God who created man planned from all Eternity the redemption of man. St. John tells us, that "God so loved the world as to give His only begotten Son" and the Son so loved us as to give Himself for our salvation. And immediately on earth, there was the vocation of helping Jesus Christ. That help was foreshadowed in the Old Testament. Indeed, from the beginning of the race, there were men who felt drawn apart and whom God drew apart to speak to Him and honor Him and offer sacrifice to Him. But we are not concerned now with the priesthood of the Old Testament. We are concerned with the priesthood of the New Testament, with the priesthood of Jesus Christ.

Now, what is the basic plan of God? The Incarnation; that His Son without ceasing to be God should become one of us and so in the marvelous graciousness of God, as one woman had brought disgrace upon the whole human race and had opened the top, as it were, of a Pandora's box to allow evil to come into the world, so God looked upon His beautiful image of woman and her disgrace and humiliation. He undid that. He raised her up again by choosing to open the gates of life everlasting through a woman, through Mary. As one woman undid the happiness of God, the second woman would help the second Adam bind up the wounds and open wide the gates by her Son. . . *Per Christum Dominum Nostrum.*

Thus we have in Christ the beginning of a second vocation, beyond the universal vocation we all have of being called by creation to serve God as human beings. This second vocation began at the Last Supper when Our Lord ordained His first priests. Why?

To pave the way for the continuation of the Incarnation to the end of time. Mary, the Virgin, brought Him into the world and clothed Him with her flesh. It was His intention to be in the world until the end of time. "I will not leave you orphans. . . I will come to you. . . Behold I am with you all days even to the consummation of the world." How was this to be accomplished?

He showed how it was to be accomplished when on the threshold of His Passion, He took the bread and wine, transubstantiated them into His Body and Blood, and then turning to His newly to be ordained priests, He said: "Do this in commemoration of Me," and by those very words ordained them.

In other words, He established another vocation on earth, the tremendous vocation of helping Jesus Christ save mankind; and at the very heart is that vocation in which you participate by your total dedication and consecration and oblation to Our Lord. Our Blessed Lord set at the heart of that vocation His priests, for as the heart in the physical unity and entity of man keeps the blood pulsating to all parts of the body and receives it back again purified, so the priest of God by the pulsation of the words of the consecration of his Mass effects that the Blood of Jesus Christ shall be on earth and shall go forth through the arteries of the sacramental life of the Church; and in the mysterious ways of Divine Grace for the purification of the whole Mystical Body, which we are in God's Holy Spirit.

What are we saying? Are we saying that the priest, offering Mass for us this morning here at the altar, gave to you the same Jesus Christ that Mary gave to the whole world by her unique maternity? Yes!

So the priest by the Consecration of his Mass supplied Jesus Christ and all the priests saying Mass this morning and every morning supply Jesus Christ to the children of men.

Now that involves the coming of Jesus Christ to a real but mystical sacrifice, the Sacrifice of the Mass, in which all the merit of His bloody sacrifice on Calvary is made available to the children of men, in which He continues ceaselessly, for Masses are being said somewhere in the world at every hour. So unceasingly, Jesus Christ has found through His priests, a way to continue His life of sacrifice. He can no longer suffer, but His priests can suffer for Him.

Therefore, you see how natural and logical it is that, as in the sacrament of matrimony, when a husband and wife dedicate their bodies and souls exclusively to God and their partnership in God, to work with Him for the creation and training and care of little ones, so how logical it is and what has taken place through the Christian centuries, that the mind of the Spirit of God is expressed in the discipline of God's Church, which asks a man who aspires to this vocation to walk as Christ did without a home of his own and to be so in love with the heart of humanity, that he would not give himself exclusively to any one heart, except the Heart of Christ in the Blessed Sacrament and the Heart of the Mother of God, to whom it is safe for all of us to give our hearts.

You see the beautiful unfolding of the plan. That is why I have been able to say that God's greatest gift to man is the priesthood, because it gives Christ day by day to mankind. It makes it possible for you to come in here at midnight and find Jesus Christ waiting here for you. It is responsible for your own vocation. You are here because Jesus is here and Jesus would not be here unless a priest had consecrated a Host at Mass.

The second part of Father Gerald's two superlatives follows logically from the first. If the highest of God's grace to us is His priesthood, then the highest form of generosity we can give to God is to correspond with the grace of the priesthood.

We must remember that God and God's grace will never do violence to a human soul. God respects the gift of liberty that He has created. He even inspires parents to recognize this freedom in the children from their earliest days.

A good Christian mother, as she picks up her little one, would say: "Would my little boy like to get up now?" The child might not want to, but at least he says so. She will try to persuade him if he does not. There is respect for the liberty of the individual; that little sovereignty God has established in the soul.

God invites His creatures in the Church today to participate in His life, in the Life of the Adorable Trinity. The vast majority of men and women feel drawn, unless there are some circumstances that prevent it in their life; some obvious obligation like that of a good daughter, who stays at home to take care of her mother, or a son in the family, who sacrifices himself and gives up the establishment of a home of his own because there is no one to take care of the aged parents. The beautiful Providence of God, which extends to every slightest detail of our lives, governs that.

There is no real lasting happiness without discipline in every vocation. Thus we see how God has provided for the happiness of married people through their cooperation with His grace in the sacrament of matrimony.

But here and there, God whispers to a boy, a young man, or a widower, a man in mature life — "Come and help Me and I will make you fishers of men." "Come and walk alone with Me, that I may have the opportunity by your annihilation that Christ shall live in you." And so you have the equivalent of the transubstantiation in the ideal accomplished by the grace of God.

Our Lord is completely dedicated to helping us. What He does, He does with absolute generosity. You have the proof of that in daily Communion for He just doesn't shake hands with you. No, it is the whole Christ who comes to us in the fullness of His divinity and humanity, with His body and soul, entering our body and soul.

And so it is with that other mystical taking over, possession. God wants by grace to transubstantiate His creations until He can say with St. Paul and with all the priests saying to God — "I live now, not I, but Christ lives in me."

So the priest in the ideal fulfillment of his vocation must not only speak the words that turn the bread and wine into

the Body and Blood of Christ, but he must permit himself
to be transubstantiated, so he can say by the grace of God:
"I live now not I, but Christ lives in me."

That is why, let me say in closing, I believe I am justified
in saying that the priesthood is God's greatest gift to man
because it gives us Christ in the world today. Its faithful
fulfillment is man's greatest gift to God because the priesthood not only gives Christ to man, but gives Christ to God.

In giving Christ to God, it is not only giving the sacramental Christ, but Christ in you. It takes Christ to those
dying and able to receive the Last Sacraments. The priest
comes and gives Christ to the dying Christians. First of
all, he washed that soul in the Blood of Christ in the Sacrament of Penance. He gives it, as it were, a baptism for
eternal life in the Sacrament of Anointing. Finally, in Holy
Viaticum, he gives the soul Christ and he makes it possible for the soul to give itself to Christ washed and purified and sanctified in the Blood of the Lamb, so that at
that moment on the threshold of Eternity, having seen that
it was safe in the arms of Christ, we might logically say:
"Oh, my Jesus, I thank you for the priesthood by which
you came to me and I have come safely to you."[1]

What is Father Gerald saying? He is setting down the two basic
ideas that should motivate every Catholic believer: gratitude to God
for giving us the priesthood, and concern to make sure that priests
are faithful to their sublime vocation.

To be told that, "the priesthood is God's greatest gift to man,"
does not mean merely that the priesthood is the highest calling a
human being can receive from God. More than that, as the continu-
ance of the Incarnation, it is the highest benefit that God, become
man, has bestowed on the human race.

Running as a theme throughout his conferences and the foundation of all his apostolic labors was this sense of gratitude that Father Gerald wished to inspire in every believer: God not only became
man but He remains man; and as man Christ offers Himself to the
Father in the Mass, comes to us in Holy Communion, and lives among

us in the Holy Eucharist — through the priesthood which He instituted at the Last Supper.

But gratitude for the priesthood must be more than sterile sentiment. It should manifest itself in deeds; priests are to live up to their awesome responsibility.

Everything that Father Gerald said or wrote on the subject — by now in thousands of words; and everything he did *Pro Christo Sacerdote*, for Christ the Priest — was somehow an expression of these two principles, like two pillars, on which he built: gratitude and faithfulness.

What bears emphasis, however, is that the duty of thankful fidelity is a two-edged sword. It applies mainly to the priest himself, but not only. The People of God are all beneficiaries of the priesthood. They also have the duty to show their appreciation for this divine gift and, by prayer and sacrifice, to help priests remain faithful to their sublime destiny.

III. The Virtues of a Priest

It is not surprising that the man who spent so many years laboring to bring priests back to the fold should have much to say about the virtues of a priest. We might almost say that this was the substance of all he had to say.

Father Gerald was convinced that, given their indispensable role in the Church of God, as the ones who bring Christ down on earth in the Eucharist, and the ministers of the sacraments and the Word, priests must above all be holy men. Behind this conviction was the memory of the Church's long history. Holy priests sanctify their people; unholy priests, except for a miracle of grace, turn people away from God. "It is true," he admitted, "that no soul in all the world will be lost without its own deliberate and consummate folly." Granting this, yet for "the soul in a parish where there is a saintly priest, his chances are multiplied a thousand fold. The young people who fall under the influence of a holy priest, how they are strengthened to meet the temptations and dangers of the world for all their life. God, after His own self, after His own incarnate self, has no more powerful means of saving souls than His priests. As a matter of fact, He counts upon His priests to give His sacramental Self to the Mystical Body."[1]

This was the underlying principle of Father Gerald's work of priestly rehabilitation. It takes priests to restore holiness among priests who have drifted away. Indeed, it takes exceptionally holy priests to do this. Hence the towering importance of holiness in those who would sanctify their fellow priests.

> When we sanctify priests, when we put them back and make them what they ought to be, we are making the most vital contribution to the salvation of man and thus to the glory of God that can be made on earth. Let me repeat

29

that statement: Priests who devote themselves to the sanctification of their fellow priests, and of course this implies sanctifying themselves as Our Lord Himself said: to sanctify Himself for their sake and for the sake of others. He had the fullness of sanctification but He went through the life and the fast and the prayer and the vigils and the Apostolic labors, personal demonstrations, for the sake of His brethren, for the sake of His Priests.

The priest who devotes himself to the sanctification of his fellow priests is making a most direct and most vital contribution to the salvation of man and thus the glory of God that can be made on earth.[2]

One of Father Gerald's favorite patrons was the Cure of Ars, who, he said, "made thousands of priests holy men, fervent priests." Father Gerald's idea was to follow the same philosophy. "I was anxious to do as much as I could for the Sacred Heart, and I asked myself: What is the most efficient way of helping the Sacred Heart? And the answer of course is obvious: Sanctify my priests. If we can sanctify priests for Christ, then we are opening up the God-chosen channels of sanctification for others, for the whole world, for the Church, for the Mystical Body."[3]

Here was the motivation he urged on everyone who would listen, priests, religious and the laity. Work, pray and sacrifice for the sanctification of priests and you are engaged in the fundamental apostolate of the Catholic Church.

FAITH IN THE EUCHARIST

At the bedrock of the Christian religion is faith. Without faith there can be no pleasing God. "It is true we're going to be judged by charity, and especially the works of fraternal charity, the corporal works of mercy. But the man who performs the corporal works of mercy in a salvific manner is dominated by faith. He cannot receive credit from God except for that which is done by faith. 'For without faith, it is impossible for a man to please God.'" (Hebrews 11:6).[4]

What is true of Christians in general is also and emphatically true of priests. Their supernatural faith is what makes them acceptable to God.

But the function of faith in a priest lies deeper still. In Father Gerald's estimation, it was not just faith as such, but faith in the Eucharist that first led a young man to aspire to the priesthood.

It is our faith in the Blessed Sacrament that was responsible for most of our vocations, probably all our vocations. We became priests because of the Mass, or because of the divine-abiding presence in the Sacrament of love. Many vocations have their source; if they could be analyzed and studied, we would find that they amounted to this formula: I believe that the Son of God has made Himself a prisoner of love in this little white Host in this tabernacle for me. He who is my God, loves me enough to be here as a prisoner of love, then I love Him enough to give up the joys and consolations of a Christian home and be His prisoner of love. A good priest is a prisoner of love of our Lord because our Lord is a prisoner of love for him. And in proportion that his faith is living, he has that consolation.[5]

Again and again, Father Gerald returns to the same idea: "Faith is what led us into the most sublime of all our possessions, our priesthood. It was our faith (especially in the Real Presence; faith in what it meant to be a priest, to be in that relationship to the Son of God) that was at the bottom of and basic, under God, to our vocation."

So true is this that, after years of experience with wayward shepherds, Father Gerald reached a conclusion that deserves to be etched in bronze. "The most difficult cases we shall ever deal with in our apostolate will not be priests who are sinners but priests who have lost the faith."[6] As later events were to prove, the most intractable persons to cope with, and they can be very learned, are men who had once believed in the Real Presence, and therefore in the priesthood, but lost faith in the Eucharist and therefore lost their sense of identity as priests.

It was, no doubt, symbolic of what was later to occur in his life, that Father Gerald recalled with gratitude that, "the greatest happiness I have in thirty-four years in the priesthood is the knowledge that I spent the afternoon of my ordination largely with Jesus Christ. I didn't know Him so well then as I know Him now, but I did know enough that I was ordained to serve and love the King of Kings. That's faith. My love is very far from being perfect, but I have faith."[7]

This deep faith, centering on the Eucharist, Father Gerald tried by all means to inspire, or arouse, in other priests. Certainly in working with other shepherds, "we must have faith, or we cannot help these priests who come to us."[8]

It follows, then, that if faith is so important, a priest should pray daily to deepen his faith. He recommended that "every time in the Mass that we say the Credo, we ask God to strengthen our faith." Priests should daily make "an act of gratitude to God and a petition to God to strengthen our faith that, come what may, we, like St. Teresa of Avila, will be able to say when we're dying, 'Thank God I die a child of the Faith, a daughter of the Faith,' and me, a priest of God, I die in my faith."[9]

HUMILITY OF MIND AND HEART

Building on faith in God's revelation, especially in the Eucharist, a priest must cultivate deep interior humility.

Why is humility so necessary in the life of a priest? Because without this virtue there is no possibility of growing in intimacy with Christ. "I cannot be a favorite of the Sacred Heart, I cannot be an intimate of the Sacred Heart, I cannot be one of those who are close to the Sacred Heart, unless I achieve humility."[10]

This stands to supernatural reason. If God resists the proud and gives His grace to the humble, how can a proud priest expect to grow in holiness without grace, if he cannot receive the grace without humility? It took the humiliation of God to teach us, especially priests, humility.

What is most necessary for the priestly heart? To do that which is so difficult for man and so easy for God. Do we see the Apostles during the three years of the public life, do we see them at any one scene prostrate at Our Lord's feet? Not until the Resurrection. Only one of them was at Calvary; none of them were at Bethlehem. But we see the reverse, we see at the Last Supper the Sacred Heart of Jesus actually in the person of Christ, in the framework of

His humanity, kneeling at the feet of His disciples. O my God why have we the need of going any further to learn the lesson of humility? The heart of God at the feet of His disciples! And apparently only one of them, only Peter, saw the incongruity, at least expressed the incongruity: Thou shall never wash my feet. Get up Lord and let me kneel and wash your feet. And then the lesson: Unless I wash you, you shall have no part with Me. And unless you wash us, beloved Jesus, unless you had humbled yourself, what chance of conversion would there be for our proud hearts? What is all pride and especially what is pride in a priestly heart but a heart lifting itself and saying: I will be a god unto myself and of myself. *Non serviam* — I will not serve.[11]

Not only is pride sinful, but it is most unreasonable. It is surely a mystery of life why anyone should be proud. And can any person who is proud ever be happy? Pride is so obviously a source of anguish.

For the proud heart is not at peace, even with itself. The proud heart partakes in some mysterious manner of the everlasting perturbation and anguish of Lucifer. There is no peace in hell because there is nothing but pride in hell. There can be no peace in a priestly heart while the thorn of pride is there. Humility is always beautiful to God. Cultivate it with that simplicity of purpose: This is the thing that will make me most pleasing to God. "Learn of Me for I am meek and humble of heart." If you can be humble you can be a saint.[12]

How is humility to be understood? It is to be seen in two phases. The first phase is a recognition of my own nothingness, that, except for God, I would not even exist, and, except for His sustaining hand, I should relapse into the nothingness from which I came. The second phase is the willingness to be treated for what, of myself, I really am, nothing.

Take the priest at the altar, who begins the Mass by admitting his sins. Suppose, after Mass, he is accused of something he has done wrong. "How few priests, when brought face to face with an accusation, even true, will respond humbly and will say quietly, 'I'm sorry, but I was at fault in that case," and will do it without rancor and with simplicity of spirit? It is one thing to acknowledge our nothingness to God, and it is another thing to accept that same evaluation from our fellow man."[13]

If humility is always desirable, it is indispensable for successful work with persons — especially priests — who have fallen. That is why Father Gerald literally begged, "I beg you, dear Fathers," he told his priests, "to cultivate humility after charity itself." Then he explained.

> Humility is really a form of charity, for us anyway, for if we are humble we will be charitable. We shall be considerate for the falls of others. We can understand how a man can fall, and fall and fall, and if we can't understand it, we can be patient with it, for this condition. This is why God can draw good out of evil. Even in our own falls and frailties and our infidelities to our Lord. The man who has never failed God is in great danger — in great natural danger of pride. He is very apt to be like the Pharisee who stands and says: I am not like the rest of men. We cannot help our fellow priests here in this canyon, in our Apostolate, without being personally men of humility, grounded in humility, fastened in humility permanently. It would be my honest conclusion that eighty-five percent, perhaps even more, ninety-five percent of the problems that bring priests to Via Coeli have their root in pride. A proud man will not stop following his course of folly; a humble man will learn even by his mistakes. A proud man will not learn; he refuses to learn even from his mistakes. A humble man, if he offends God, no matter in what virtue it may be, will come back to his God and say: I'm sorry. The proud man cannot say: I'm sorry. Because pride is self-deification.[14]

How to cultivate humility? By reflecting on God's humility, in the Incarnation, and in the Blessed Sacrament. Could God have humbled Himself more than to hide His divinity to assume our humanity; and then, as man, to even hide His humanity under the sacramental veils of the Eucharist?

Here the God who owns all things beyond the ownership of men, who owns everything and brought everything out of His creative power, who owns everything by the right of creation, is "pauper." He who controls the unthinkable powers of the atom — all rests at the fingertips of His will — all atomic energy — all energy that is or ever will be or ever has been or ever could be — the sum total, here He is in the frailty of the little wheaten host. He whom the heavens cannot contain, imprisons Himself in a little brass circle, gold-plated or silver — what does it matter? He created both silver and gold — and earth and spirit — and He created me and I owe Him everything.[15]

How further to cultivate humility? By praying and asking God and His Mother to make us humble. A suggested prayer: "O God, if for one minute, one split second, you were to put the power of God in my power, it would be my happiness to return it to you so that you could say that you had permitted a creature to be in a position to dethrone you and the creature, like our Blessed Mother, had refused to usurp the power of God." Priests should cultivate this attitude: "Humble yourselves in private prayer before our dear Lord. What graces He will flood into your souls. Our Blessed Mother revealed this when she said: Because He has regarded the lowliness, the humility of His handmaid. Annihilate yourself and God will fill yourself with His Divine and True Self, for He alone IS. And from time to time repeat this which is a favorite ejaculation of my own: Let this be not forgot, dear Lord, let this be not forgot: Thou art and I am not."[16]

CHRISTLIKE CHARM

The charity of a priest should affect his whole life. People should see in him something of the love that Christ had for others, especially for those who were, humanly speaking, least deserving of love. This charity ought to be shown, above all, in priestly friendship.

To be the friend of Christ involves being a friend to those round about us, even when that is inconvenient from an earthly point of view. If we are to love our neighbor as Jesus loves us we must love him even when our neighbor is unlovable. Is it not true that Christ has loved us in our unlovableness? That is the wonderment of Divine Love.

That is the reason of our Apostolate — to love those who have been unworthy of His love. He loved them and He loves us when we are unlovable. And believe me, even consecrated souls, even priests can be terribly unlovable.

Remember that our Lord very carefully pins down who are His true disciples. They are those who are set upon deliberately loving their neighbor as Christ has loved us. How has Christ loved us? He has loved us to the point of sacrifice. He has loved us to the point of giving His life for us and we must love our neighbor to the point of laying down our lives in the fulfillment of our vocation. We must love God's priests even when they are unlovable. Now that does not mean being weak with them. God has not been weak with us. At times in His love for us, He has dealt with a strong and firm hand but always it was motivated, not with impatience, but because He wished us not to lose Him for eternal life. He wanted us to be with Him for all eternity, and so He sought us in our weakness. He sought us in our difficulties. He sacrificed Himself for us.[17]

One of the greatest trials of the priesthood, as only a man like Father Gerald would know, was loneliness. And one of the main reasons for loneliness, he was convinced, was the lack of selfless friendship among priests. That is why he stressed so much the practice of kindness and forbearance, if need be to heroism, with men who were often victims of failure in Christian charity. "We can always find good in human nature," he insisted. "By cultivating, by noticing the good we can encourage others to build that good up."[18] And again, "If we could only remember. If we could only ask ourselves: Have I permitted myself to wound a fellow priest, or anyone?"[19]

Given his exposure to human weakness and his familiarity with human sin, "One of the most essential virtues of a priest, essential for the fulfillment of his vocation is the capacity for silence. If one stops to reflect, it will become increasingly evident. One has to be like God, and I say that reverently, like God who knows all things, and yet who is so slow to reveal the humiliations of the individual to his fellows."

Recall what happened at the Last Supper. When Judas had planned to betray the Savior, and he was about to carry the betrayal into effect, what did Jesus do? He did not reveal the betrayer. Instead, He cryptically told the disciples that one of them was a devil. But when asked "Who?" He did not identify Judas. Finally, in Gethsemane, the traitor betrayed himself.

> There is a dreadful, terrible possibility that flows from that forbearance and silence of God. A priest can go to the altar for years and Jesus Christ will not betray him, can go to the altar in mortal sin and God will not betray him. O dear Fathers, what a tremendous forbearance, what a tremendous self-control the Son of God is exercising! Not only 1900 years ago at the Last Supper, but in the world today. And that is one reason why to men of faith, we do not need to go backwards through the centuries. Today is the Passion! Today. We know because we have cared for souls. We know today somewhere in the world Judas' lips met our Lord; somewhere in the world our Lord whispered to a poor soul, both souls of laity and souls of priests, "Dost thou betray the Son of God with a kiss?" "And Jesus was silent." Today.[20]

Practicing charity by keeping silence is "especially necessary for us in the fulfillment of our vocation because we like Peter and John become aware of the sorrows of the Sacred Heart." In the priesthood, "we become aware of the humiliations, the humiliating failures and sins of priests. How careful we must be."

As Father Gerald saw the failures of priests, they are humiliations to the Heart of Christ. The devil taunts the Savior with that. To point up what this means, he recalled the example of Job in the Scriptures. God spoke of His servant Job, who always praised the Divine Majesty, to Lucifer, and Lucifer said, "Let me have him; let me have a chance at him and we'll see whether he will or not."

> Therefore, when we avoid speaking unnecessarily of the faults and failures of a priest, we are saving the Sacred Heart from being reminded of something that has been a humiliation and by anticipation something He has already

suffered for, something that brought the dew of Blood to
His forehead and face in the Garden of Gethsemane. There
is not one of us who has not heard sufficient confessions
to understand why Jesus sweat Blood in the Garden of
Gethsemane.[21]

There is another reason, however, why a priest should keep
discreetly silent about what he knows are the sins of others, including
his fellow-priests. This is the motive that Christ went out of His
way to emphasize, namely to obtain mercy for oneself. The Beati-
tude, "Blessed are the merciful, for they shall obtain mercy," is no
mere option. It is a grave obligation. It is also a salutary following of
Christ. "If we imitate the Sacred Heart of Jesus, if we hide the faults
and failings, even the serious failings, speaking only when it is necessary for the guidance and the help of a soul, shall we not qualify
for the mercy of God?" Needless to say, "We're not looking for the
justice of God. It is too sharp a sword. We want the mercy of the
Sacred Heart. Very well. Let us be merciful. Let us even avoid thinking of the sins of men and especially the sins of priests."[22]

Father Gerald was too wise to suppose this meant stultifying
one's intelligence or closing one's eyes to the obvious. But it is one
thing to recognize evil when faced with sin, and being overwhelmed
even by the enormity of some crime, and dwelling on the sins of others
or talking about them as a sort of pastime or thus inflating one's ego.
Imitating the charitable "silence of Jesus Christ is never vacuity. It does
not mean and is not the silence of the dotage of old age; it is not the
silence of the moron. It is a silence that is eloquent with the realization
of the Presence of God,"[23] who is love, and who, out of love, passes
over in silence (without condoning) the failures of His creatures.

GENEROSITY OF SPIRIT

The practice of charity is already high virtue, and its presence
in a priest is one of the marks of his nearness to God. But generosity
of spirit, if possible, goes beyond charity. Or rather it is a perfection
of charity that not only looks for the good in others to praise them,
but seeks out the needs of others to meet them.

The measure of your greatness, dear Fathers, if you want
a practical measure of your spiritual stature, you will find

it in terms of your generosity. How generous you are. And remember, to us, our Lord has said: Generously you have received. And who has received more generously from God, than the priest of God?[24]

Immediately, however, as we speak of generosity, we must carefully distinguish between two types of souls, even generous souls. This classification is not arbitrary. "It is according to the generosity of the soul, whether of priest, religious, or the lay person."

> There are good souls, but the good souls whose goodness is very well concerned with their own immediate peace and happiness. They belong to God: they abide in God but they do not sacrifice much to God: they are pleasing to God, they are acceptable to God, they belong to God but they are not upon the Cross with Christ. At most they are bearing witness from a distance. There are other souls who deliberately draw close to the Cross of Christ. And even by the generosity of their spirit and the persistency of their sacrifice invite our Lord to come down and let them take His place on the Cross. Our Lord never does come down from the Cross. He didn't until He was dead. Even when He was tempted humanly speaking to do so and to put at naught His enemies, "Come down from the Cross and we will acknowledge you." We acknowledge you Jesus because you did not come down from the Cross: we acknowledge you as the King of love, unselfish love. But there was another heart at the foot of the Cross that was inviting our Lord to come down; in fact there were three hearts that were inviting our Lord to come down from the Cross: one was the heart of His Mother, one was the heart of His priest, one was the heart of His penitent, Magdalen.[25]

Speaking to priests, Father Gerald began with an invocation, "O Lord, Jesus, how fortunate we are." Then a plea for priestly generosity: "The heart of John can be our heart because we are Thy priests," of whom Christ expects more than of others. "The heart of Magdalen belongs to us because we too have offended Thee grievously and therefore we belong to the penitent, the penitent heart is ours," ready to give much to others because so much has been mercifully given to us. "And we belong to the Immaculate Heart of Mary because to the heart of a priest and the heart of a penitent, the Heart of the Mother of God belongs," and she knows how to inspire her Son's priests to give after the example of her Son who died on the Cross to expiate our sins.

If a person, and especially a priest, is generous, he will also be zealous. Generosity without zeal is spurious, even as zeal without generosity is self-seeking.

The great exemplar of generous, apostolic zeal was St. Paul, whom Father Gerald never tires presenting to priests as a model for their imitation. As we review the history of the Apostle we are struck by the logic of God's Providence.

There was first of all the man himself, Saul, on whose ardent nature the Lord decided to build the edifice of His grace. "What is characteristic of Paul and what we need today to stem the terrible tide of worldliness that is sweeping in on the Church, is this energetic approach — St. Paul was a man of energy. He was not big physically but he was big in the sense of the flaming intensity of his soul. Whatever he would do he would do intensely; and so when he started to persecute the Church he did it intensely: he was following through. When finished cleaning up the Christians in Jerusalem, he was going up to Damascus to bring them back for trial. He made a crusading district attorney."[26]

So much for nature. "And then someone interfered. Then the Master stopped him in his tracks on his way to Damascus. Let us not forget that after Christ Himself, there has not been a more momentous moment for the Church than that moment when Jesus stopped a fiery little man bent upon persecution of Christ's followers."

In entering the life of Saul, Christ did more than convert him from prosecutor to apostle. He enlightened Saul on the two facts of faith that should dominate the life of every priest, that God became Man and dwells among us, and that this God-man identifies the faithful with Himself, so that whatever is done for them (in charity) or against them (in malice) Christ takes as being done to Himself.

Saul was changed to Paul by the grace of Jesus. "From that moment that most startling and most redeeming revelation of Divine Love dominated this man, of magnificent mind and soul. Would to God that the same had been true and was true of every priest."[27]

How the Church needs priests with something of the burning zeal of the Apostle. What she needs is more men like him.

What could stop the conquest of the Holy Spirit if every priest was Pauline in his spirit? What could stop us? Think of the agony of the Sacred Heart who can find so few priests who go all out for Him, their God who goes all out for us.[28]

Father Gerald was fond of quoting the words of the devil from the lips of a possessed person to the Cure of Ars who had taken 80,000 souls from him. Then the devil is supposed to have added, "If there were three more priests like you in the world, my kingdom would be destroyed."

The lesson of this was clear. The Cure of Ars was a zealous priest. He spent long hours in the confessional reconciling sinners with God. But behind those sixteen and more hours a day listening to sins was the zeal of a great lover of God. "Before he died, forty, fifty thousand were coming every year to go to confession to him." They were drawn by his sanctity and the wisdom that holy priests invariably receive from God.

As we look around us today, what is the picture we see? "The Sacred Heart, from all His thousands of priests, can only find a handful who are ready to be so completely inebriated with His Spirit as was the Cure of Ars. Dear Fathers, I would wish you to be ambitious men, ambitious for just one thing, for loving Christ as He has never been loved before" — and showing this love by spending oneself in zealous advancement of Christ's Kingdom on earth.

IV. We Can Achieve
What We Will

One evidence of Father Gerald's balanced spirituality is the fact that he never lost sight of the human factor in the pursuit of sanctity. He never tired of urging priests to pray. And all we have so far seen should make it clear that he looked to divine grace for whatever success a person expects in the ways of God.

At the same time, he had no illusions about God's expectations of man. If we are to pray and beg the divine mercy for help, as though everything depended on Him, we are also to exert ourselves as though everything depended on us.

Father Gerald used the apostles often to illustrate his teaching of priests, and for the present purpose he found the combination of Matthias and Judas especially instructive. Matthias was chosen to replace Judas because Judas had freely decided to betray the Master. Matthias, therefore, exemplifies one of the great fundamentals in the priestly life, the fact of human liberty. "We cannot think of St. Matthias without thinking of Judas who could have been a saint; but he did not want to."

> Before us in our individual souls is set the tremendous privilege, the tremendous reality of the liberty of our individual free will. We *can achieve what we will*. We can become saints of God. We can make a tremendous contribution individually to the application of the generosity of Divine Love as waiting for man in the Divine Treasury of the Sacred Heart. God's desire is to save and sanctify mankind. He could have done it all alone but there cer-

tainly is a certain reasonableness that God should call upon His Image to cooperate in the salvation of others.[1]

In one sense, every human being who has reached the age of reason is thus called to cooperate, not only in his own salvation but in the salvation of others. We are our brothers' and sisters' keepers. But from the dawn of salvation history, some people are called to a special, and more intimate, cooperation with the salvific plan of God: the ancient patriarchs Abraham, Isaac and Jacob; then Moses and Aaron; and after them all the prophets, from the great ones like Isaiah and Jeremiah, to the lesser ones like Nahum and Osee. Without exception, they were chosen by Yahweh to be His spokesmen, through no merit of their own, but only because they were to be the channels of His will and the instruments of His grace to the People of Israel.

With the coming of Christ, there was no change in the divine economy of salvation. What the patriarchs and prophets were in the Old Law, the apostles and their successors — on a higher and more sublime level — became in the New Dispensation. It is in this context that bishops and priests become part of God's mysterious Providence.

He has invited us from among all the thousands of mankind. He has called upon priests to help Him in the salvation of our fellow men. O Lord what a privilege. Thou who art God hast invited me a little creature to come and help You to save the world. Why? That is veiled in the mysterious depths of Thy predilection and of Thy love, for when God calls a man to a special service, He does so out of love. We see that most clearly illustrated in the story of a young man who did not answer that call. The young man who asked our Lord: What must I do to gain eternal life? And our Lord said to him: Keep the commandments. And he said with simplicity: All these I have done since my youth. And our Lord looked upon his soul and it is said that our Lord loved him, and He said: If thou wouldst be perfect, go sell what thou hast and come follow me. . . an invitation. And the young man went away sorrowing because he had many possessions. But our Lord's love was the source of the call. . . He looked upon him and loved him and He called him.

And so our dear Lord looked upon our souls very early and perhaps revealed His love only when we were comparatively mature. He looked upon us and loved us and called us. And that same love, because it is His love, is still anxious to have us fulfill our first vocation. And not only fulfill it but gives us a unique privilege of extending the invitation of love to those who have betrayed our Lord.[2]

While these words were originally spoken to the Paracletes, whom Father Gerald was training for work among stray shepherds, they apply with equal vigor to all priests. They are all chosen by the Savior to labor with Him in reconciling sinners with their Creator. But the degree of their priestly zeal depends on how clearly they recognize their own indispensable role, as, *willing agents* in the hands of a merciful God. "He has actually made us free," either to respond to His vocation or refuse to follow Him in the priesthood; and again either to generously cooperate with the Savior in the priestly apostolate or selfishly hold back. Father Gerald was speaking in 1955 when he declared that, "we are approaching a time in the world when there is a subtle propaganda to destroy the actual recognition of free will."[3] The social and psychological sciences are conspiring to reduce man to a mere robot, and his actions to the product of heredity, environment and education. On these premises, Christianity becomes a myth and the function of sacraments and the priesthood a fraud. What Father Gerald saw here was the modern residue of what in the sixteenth century invaded the Western world as Calvinism. But Calvinism then and determinism today are not true. They are in open contradiction to the whole message of the Gospels, and priests had better awaken to the danger that faces modern man under the guise of emancipating him.

The whole philosophy of the Son of God dying means that He was trying to reach their free will: He is appealing to their free will. He is recognizing their free will and supplying a motive to entice the free will of man by the movement of grace of course to submit their will to God freely and thus enter into eternal life. "Not everyone who says to me, Lord, Lord, shall enter into my heavenly Kingdom, but he who does the will of my Father." He who substitutes the will of God for his own little will shall enter into the Kingdom. The choice is reserved to each individual soul. Before man are two highroads — the highroad of God's beautiful will and the highroad of his own will and every man including every priest makes choice of which way he will travel. Therefore, if God has elected us, we must ratify that election and for God, we must choose God. So great is the independence of God in us, the liberty of God in us that God solicits as a lover asks for a lover's consent for a marriage contract, so our Lord tells us: Behold I stand at the door and knock. Notice He doesn't force His way in. He doesn't break in. He waits for the door to be opened at His knock. He waits for man to correspond with His grace, to ratify the choice that God is offering him.[4]

The implications of this philosophy are far-reaching. Contrary to the world's philosophy, that is forever talking about freedom, while denying it in practice, the philosophy of Christ recognizes that we are free human beings, capable of either loving God by doing His will, or rejecting God by doing our own will in contradiction to His.

It must seem ironical for Father Gerald to be so insisting on human freedom in directing priests, when the popular image of a priest is of one whose main role is to inhibit human freedom by telling people what they are obliged or forbidden to do.

But that is precisely where the error of modern amorality needs to be exposed. Critics of the Church, or of the priesthood, when it is faithful to Christ, forget that the whole of God's law is an expression of God's love. He forbids and commands us not to inhibit our liberty but to keep us truly free by doing, not what we please, but what He knows will make us happy, both now and in eternity. Once this fact dawns on a person, he will respond with "a lover's consent" to what God "solicits as a lover" from His creatures.

If a priest needs to keep the beauty of human freedom always before his eyes, and never tire of teaching it to others, he must also remember that his own will has been weakened by sin and therefore needs constant strengthening by self-denial and prayer. Never forget that "the will is strengthened by exercising it, just as the will is weak-

ened by the failure to exercise it." This simple truth put into practice
produces saints.

> Watch a football squad that trains zealously — they do
> this to give themselves strength and ability when the real
> contest comes. If we do not deny ourselves the little things,
> if we do not in the secret of our own little hidden life
> exercise, *agere contra*, our will will grow flabby and then
> some day when a major assault is made against the will,
> we will not be prepared. Peter failed our Lord when he
> had permitted himself the indulgence of warming his fin-
> gers, a very simple and little indulgence, but was it in keep-
> ing when the Son of God was mocked and spat upon and
> insulted? It was an act of self-indulgence that took Peter
> off his guard and made it possible for a strong courageous
> man to become a liar and a traitor to his Master.

> Quietly, each in your own way, strengthen your wills, dear
> Fathers. Keep back the little word, keep back the little
> taste of satisfaction of some appetite, curb the little bit of
> mental or physical curiosity, exercise in a hidden way your
> will in "agere contra" the natural satisfactions of life. And
> what comes from that? When the time comes for the Mas-
> ter to ask you to ascend the Cross with Him, you will be
> prepared. The man who does not die to self every day, in
> the little things, will not be able in the end to die to self in
> the greater things without some special dispensation of
> divine Mercy.[5]

There is more here than meets the eye. For one who believes in
Christ and is a priest of God, this is not mere voluntary discipline. It
is imitation of the Master. Choose by preference until it becomes
habitual, what the Lord wants.

> Will what God wills, not only sentimentally, not only
> emotionally, not only with your lips, not only with your
> heart, but with your will, will the will of God. Go to
> Gethsemane and see there the Son of God placing Him-
> self, under emotional stress, that which alone could bring
> distress to an All-Holy Man — to be identified with the

rebellion of rebellious beings. His lips to be identified with all the lies and blasphemies and evil speaking, His hands to be identified with all the acts of impurity and violent murder. We could go on but what is the need? He flung Himself deliberately into a situation where His whole Being cried out. Because of His very holiness — strange paradox of His vocation — to become SIN to redeem sinners, to become the scapegoat. And the very moment when His whole soul revolted because of His holiness of becoming identified with sin, abandoned Himself, and as all men by the essence of their sin turn and say: I will not — to God, He said: I will. But He wanted us to know that He did it purely and completely in abandonment to the Divine Will.[6]

No one is saying this is easy, as no one claims this comes either naturally or without a struggle. But that is why Christ gave us the awesome manifestation of His humanity in the Garden of Olives. He showed that a person can be very holy and completely resigned as He was, to Divine Providence, and yet experience (at times) the agony of conflict between the indeliberate will of a creature and the manifest and demanding will of God.

One final and strong recommendation: Pray for a strong will. All that has been said so far assumes that we have the grace to do what our minds tell is plainly the will of God. But without prayer the grace will be lacking.

Dear Fathers, beg God to give you a good will. We recognize it in others, do we not? This is the great thing that we pray and hope for in the priests who come to us that we may help them here under God to rebuild their lives. We are lost, we get nowhere unless there is good will. That is all that God has blessed on earth, is it not? He made that careful distinction and had His angels express it at the moment when heaven was radiant in its own generosity, when the night was filled with the music of the angel choirs. And what is it that they are proclaiming? Not peace on earth to everyone but only peace on earth to men of good will.[7]

And what is a good will? A good will is one that is habitually disposed to do God's will. Why is it a good will? Because only in doing what God wants are we achieving what is truly good in our own lives, here and hereafter; and what is truly good for others, in terms of their best interests, even in this life and certainly in the life to come.

V. The Humanity of Christ

It is impossible to understand Father Gerald's spirituality without seeing something of his understanding of the humanity of Christ.

Somewhere near the center of this spirituality was the realization that God became man, not only to redeem a sinful race by dying on the Cross, but to show how much He loves us. Father Gerald's apostolate to priests derived from this same concentration. He saw priests as the ones who, like Mary, gave flesh to the Son of God.

When the Word of God came in the Incarnation to His Blessed Mother, He came to her first of all for her own immediate soul. "Christ loves the individual soul. He loved His Mother's soul and He came for her." But not for her alone. "He came to His Mother with intense personal love, but then He said: 'Clothe me, Mother, with your flesh, with your blood, mold me, Mother. I, the Creator who fashioned you, want you to fashion me into a man. I am the eternal Son of God; I want to be the Son of Man.' And she fashioned Him."[1]

This truth of faith is the foundation of everything else in Christianity. It is emphatically the foundation of everything distinctive in the Catholic Church. The Eucharist, Father Gerald would say, began in the womb of Mary. Unless the Son of God had taken flesh in Mary's womb there would be no Incarnation. Unless there had been an Incarnation there could not have been a Redemption. Without a Redemption no priesthood, of Christ who died on the Cross, or of others to whom Christ would communicate the power to re-enact the mystery of Calvary.

What bears emphasis, and Father Gerald never let go of this concept, is that the eternal High Priest who offers Himself in the

Mass is a true human being; that the Christ whom we receive in Holy Communion is a living human being; that the Savior who abides in our midst in the Real Presence is really present as a human being. By "human being," he understood what the Church teaches, that in the Holy Eucharist "is contained the whole Christ," and therefore with the fullness of His divinity and all the qualities of His humanity.

In the early 1940s, before he actually began his special apostolate to priests, Father Fitzgerald already had this clear vision of faith, without which everything else he said and did would have been meaningless. He saw, as few American spiritual writers in his day, that Jesus Christ is still on earth; that although He ascended to the Father and is now seated at His right hand, He did not really leave us; that His promise of not leaving us orphans meant not only that He would return at death to call us to Himself but already in life on earth He would remain in our midst.

It is literally true that, "Outside of Heaven the only place we can find the God-Man in the Sweet Humanity with which He clothed Himself, in order to be one of us, is the Blessed Sacrament."[2]

The Eucharist is called the "Blessed Sacrament" precisely because it makes sacred or sanctifies those who receive Christ's humanity. Remove this humanity and you remove sanctity from the face of the earth. Christ's presence, then, "within us" through Communion "is the fruit of His Presence on the altar, and He has told us that only by partaking of the Eucharistic Presence would the Presence by grace be renewed and revivified in us. 'Unless you eat the Flesh of the Son of Man you shall not have life in you!' Therefore here as in all else, it is the Sweet Humanity of the Son of God that nourishes the soul with the graces of which His abiding Presence is the summation. Without the Eucharist we could not abide in Jesus."[3]

GOD IS NOW MAN

It is not an uncommon temptation among spiritual persons to fancy that growth in holiness somehow means a growing independence of Christ's humanity. Nothing could be further from the truth. "Any tendency away from our Blessed Lord's Humanity it is impossible to consider as a movement into closer union either with Him or with His Heavenly Father or Sweet Holy Spirit."

Why do some people think otherwise, as we know some saints admitted? The reason may be that "we are too apt to think of Christ's Humanity as a Bridge over which one would try to pass into the Trinity," a sort of necessary convenience; so that once we cross over the bridge we can dispense with the temporary roadway. "But this concept cannot stand for Jesus has made His Humanity not a bridge," which serves a useful purpose but, once crossed, is no longer needed.

The humanity of Christ is no mere bridge to the Divinity. By the hypostatic union, Christ is permanently God made man "From the moment of the Incarnation, the Eternal Son will never be separated from His Humanity." Indeed, "even in His death on Calvary, Body and Soul were separated, yet both remained in unbroken union with His Divinity, and thus His Body in the tomb was as adorable as His Soul in Limbo." Our faith requires us to affirm that "the Son of God has entered into this ineffable Oneness with His Humanity, and has in pursuance of His Decree of everlasting union thereby lifted Himself *as Man* to the right hand of the Father and the bosom of the Eternal Trinity." Given this belief, "how foolish we would be to think that in either time or eternity we could pass beyond the warm living Heart of Christ into a more spiritual intimacy with God!" Why would this be not only foolish but false? Because "there is no intimacy with God for men except *per* (through) and *cum* (with) and, note well, *in Christo,* i.e., in Him who is everlastingly now not only God but Man."

Geraldian spirituality, if we may so call it, has its bedrock here. It is built on this premise of Christian revelation: that once God became incarnate in the womb of Mary, He has never for a moment separated Himself from this substantial, hypostatic union, to be and remain the one person, Jesus Christ, at once true God and true Man. Everything else follows on this simple mystery of the faith. God not only became man, He is man; at the Last Supper He changed bread and wine into His own Body and Blood, that is, into a living human being who is God in human form; at the same Last Supper, He gave the Apostles and their successors the power to do what He had done; as a result we now have in the Eucharist the self-same Jesus Christ who lived and died on earth, who rose from the dead and ascended into heaven — but without leaving the earth since He is literally with us in the Blessed Sacrament.

No wonder the priesthood takes on such breathtaking dignity, and priests, with all their human follies and weakness, are so important. They have the power that, by Christ's design alone, makes the continual presence of the Incarnate Son of God on earth possible.

Without the priesthood, which means, without the Eucharist, God would of course be present on earth, as He was before the Incarnation. He has to be present in the world, to sustain the world in existence and to make possible every least activity of His creatures. But, before the Incarnation and except for the Incarnation, God was and would be present on earth only *as God*. He would not, however, be present *as Man,* which means He would not have begun to exercise His mercy and love and power in human beings with that plenitude of grace that began the moment He took flesh in the body of Mary.

What He began to do at Nazareth, as soon as He took abode in His Mother's womb, God continues to do in every Nazareth in the world, which means in every place where He is now present in the Holy Eucharist.

This is the principal message of Father Gerald Fitzgerald, and whatever value his insights will have in the lives of future generations of priests and people will derive from this simple, but frequently overlooked, article of the Catholic faith.

HE IS HERE

It was this kind of literal understanding of Christ's human presence in the Eucharist that Father Gerald promoted in all his writings and conferences, not only to priests but to all the faithful. He was fully conscious of the impression he was probably having on others by teaching what must have seemed a one-sided spirituality. But he frankly did not care. "You might say that I am a fanatic," he once told the Handmaids of the Precious Blood. "I hope I am. I hope I will be recognized as a fanatic lover of the Blessed Sacrament."[4]

In season and out of season, he advocated greater attention to Christ's Real Presence by telling everyone who was willing to listen to be present to this Presence as often and for as long as possible. It simply made "supernatural sense." Father Gerald's one concern was that priests, religious and the laity would ignore the One who lived among them, and ignoring Him would fail in their love. "It is a grace," he admitted, "that God has given to me since I was a small boy to understand the reality of God's presence in the Blessed Sacrament."[5] This grace led him to the priesthood and to his Apostolate for wandering shepherds who had gone astray.

Father Gerald was sure that devotion to this Presence was the key to sound Christian living, as neglect of this Presence was the basic reason for the failures in the Christian life. "If there have been great failures among priests and religious," he declared, "it has all come about because even as yet the meaning of the Blessed Sacrament has not been comprehended. 'He comes unto His own and His own received Him not. He was in the world and the world knew Him not!'[6] This refers not only to the Jewish people at the beginning of the Christian era. It refers to believing Catholics now. In fact, "what is far sadder, we who comprehend the Blessed Sacrament, leave Our Lord alone. There is something terribly lacking. If Our Lord would be like the ordinary human being and equivalently lose His temper and raise His voice, He would say, 'What are you doing?' Are you forgetting that I am the Lord? Is work so important?'"[7] There is something wrong.

> Think of the big city parishes. Thousands of souls — how easy for the fervent pastor to arrange that the door of his church would never be locked, and that night and day this faithful would be there. Always there would be somebody with Our Lord.
>
> I was once the Curate of a little parish. Without any great difficulty we arranged that there should be a parishioner from the end of Mass in the morning until the time of locking up in the evening with Our Lord. The parishioners undertook to take one hour one day a week. And so we arranged that Our Lord should never be alone. Now is there anything more important than that?[8]

The same applies to religious communities. Writing in 1954, before the post-conciliar revolution, Father Gerald made some sage, almost prophetic observations.

All communities are crying for vocations. How the vocations would flow in where there would be perpetual Adoration of the Blessed Sacrament! How much stronger and finer and holier would be the vocations. Where can our teaching Sisters secure the spiritual energy to carry on their difficult and physically exhausting work, except by a great love for the Master in His Sacrament of Love? If the novice were made to realize the reality of the Blessed Sacrament then there would be fewer who would later fall away. Sisters would be happier because they would understand who It is who loves them.

Dear Sisters, love the Blessed Sacrament. It is the answer to everything in our lives. For a while we may be in a place where everything is very, very agreeable. But what guarantee have we? Superiors change — we may have a superior who pleases us completely, but a little telegram from the motherhouse may change it all. We must not build our lives around things that can be so quickly changed and lost. Our health, our cell, everything.

What is the one unchanging thing that we can have in our religious life? Jesus Christ in the Sacrament of His Love.[9]

The same with priests. Father Gerald makes bold to say that defections from the priesthood are mainly due to neglect of devotion to the Holy Eucharist. He goes still further to claim that, "If a priest does not love the Blessed Sacrament today he will lose his soul, or be saved only by the tremendous mercy of God and the prayers of Our Blessed Mother."

Then speaking of both vocations, it is "No wonder souls lose courage, no wonder priests and sisters fall away and turn back, seeking earthly love. They have not realized that Divine Love was so close to them."[10]

In every state of life, the secret of Christian happiness and the one means available for drawing close to God on earth as the precondition for union with Him in heaven is the God-man living and waiting for our affection in the Holy Eucharist.

The easy way to love God is in the Blessed Sacrament. What could be easier? Here is Bethlehem, here is Calvary, here is the glorious Ascension. Here is the little Christ Child climbing up on Joseph's lap to give him his morning kiss. Here is the little Christ-Child coming to His Mother and asking her to take Him into her arms and put Him to bed. Here is the great Virgin-Lover who is able as only God to give Himself whole and entire to each of us because He loves us.

What is the Blessed Sacrament? The Blessed Sacrament is All Love loving. That makes a beautiful definition of God. He needs to be our All.[11]

Addressing himself to women, whose natural affectivity would understand, but speaking through them to believers of both genders, Father Gerald could not have been plainer.

Even if you had the happiest of human homes, even if you had the greatest sense of security, the love of the finest earthly husband and children, it would only be for a few years. Your boy could be sent to war and you never see him again. Even in all your happiness could you ever have perfect happiness? Sooner or later you would know that your husband has made an appointment with a heart specialist and that he was hiding something from you. Finally you discover that he knew that he only had a certain number of years to live. The shadow of the cross lies over every life. It can't be otherwise because only by the cross can we be redeemed. And the cross is terribly hard unless we love the Corpus on it.

The Blessed Sacrament is for us the Corpus on the Cross. It is for us Mother and Father, and brother and sister, and Bridegroom and Bride. It's All. Here is all the tenderness of the Eternal Father. Here is the source of that little mysterious throbbing of your heart which means that you are living.

"O Lord Jesus, like a child who only knows that the Blessed Sacrament is Jesus, teach us that which is the supreme wisdom of all the Catholic philosophies. St. Augustine was a lover. That is the secret of sanctity, to be a lover of God. Here in the Blessed Sacrament is everything. Here is All-Love, loving."[12]

In the presence of the Real Presence, we should hold nothing back. "Bring your troubles. Bring Him your joys. Bring Him your sorrows."[13] Why? Because from Him we can receive the grace to suffer in patience and to accept His gifts in peace.

POWER GOES OUT FROM HIM

In his encyclical *The Redeemer of Man* Pope John Paul II speaks of the Eucharist as a sacrament on each of its three levels of conferring grace. "It is at one and the same time," the Pope says, "a sacrifice-sacrament, a communion-sacrament, and a presence-sacrament."[14] This means that the Eucharist is a source of supernatural enlightenment for the mind, of strength for the will when the Sacrifice of the Mass is offered, when Holy Communion is received, but also whenever the Eucharistic Lord is worshipped in His Real Presence on the altar.

This third dimension of the Eucharist as presence-sacrament was especially stressed by Father Gerald. He recognized that our first responsibility to Christ's humanity in the Eucharist should be adoration and love, as expressions of a lively faith. But the Eucharist, as Presence, is also a sacrament. It confers the grace it signifies, here the grace of power to live up to the hard demands that the Savior makes on those whom He loves. And it is the "Blessed" Sacrament because, while giving the light and strength a person needs to serve the Master, it makes this service blessed by enabling the believer to be happy in serving the one who is obeyed out of love.

But what Father Gerald never lost sight of is the power that Christ, now on earth, gives to those who in faith worship Him present in the Eucharist. Familiar passages in the Gospels about the Savior's capacity to teach and to heal are applied without apology to His continued capacity, now in the Eucharist, to do the same. When Christ said, "Behold I am with you all days, even to the consummation of the world," He meant it. "Let us put our problems away in the realization that He who is all powerful is holding us in His arms."[15] And He is here, really here in the Eucharist. "On a second occasion, He said, 'Ask the Father anything in my name, because He knows that you love me.' That's enough. When a soul goes to God that loves Jesus, it has a wide-open door into the Presence of the Adorable Trinity." Why? Because, thanks to the Eucharist, "it is already there in the Heart of Jesus Christ."[16] Consequently, "realization of the Divine Presence" in the Blessed Sacrament, "cannot be overestimated." God is here with His infinite power, as Man, ready to help us in every way. "What have we to fear?"

All of this, however, presumes what Father Gerald never tired of repeating, that the believer believes that Jesus, who is God, is present on earth and ready to work, if need be, the same miracles He worked during His visible stay in Palestine.

The capstone of this faith in the sacramental energy that emanates from Christ's humanity was clearly revealed in the miraculous healing of the woman suffering from hemorrhage for twelve years. She touched the fringe of the Savior's cloak, and the bleeding stopped at that instant. Jesus asked, "Who touched me?" When everyone around the Master denied touching Him, He insisted, "Somebody touched me. I feel that power has gone out from me." After the woman admitted having touched Jesus, He praised her, saying, "My daughter, your faith has restored you to health. Go in peace."

Provided we believe that the same Jesus is now among us, and present with the same almighty power, why should we not expect Him to work similar wonders today? "If we know how to touch the hem of Our Lord's garment in a spirit of simple faith, like the poor woman who was afflicted with an ailment, how swiftly we would be cured. This is what our Lord invites us to do. *Nolite timere* 'Don't be afraid.'"[17]

Faith generates trust, and trust is the foundation of peace. When Christ said, "Peace be with you," He meant it.

If we do not have peace, it is because we are refusing to listen to our Lord and translate our faith into a reaction which should be as simple as this, "If I had a thousand problems when I came into this church, now I haven't any because I find you here, the God who loves me and will take care of every problem of those who love you." Have complete, absolute confidence.

God requires that we believe that He is what He declares Himself to be and what we know Him to be, the Son of the Living God. "All power is given to Me in heaven and on earth." So I would recommend to you to cash in on your faith, to cash in on personal peace of soul. No harm can come to you. You belong to Jesus Christ, and how He takes care of you!

So out of the depths of your heart, just have the gratitude that should come to our heart in saying, "Well, here I am and here's my God." But since He is the physician, philosopher and the source of all healing and the beginning and end of all peace and of my journey, so if I am here, like a tired little child, I can drop my head down on the knees of Jesus Christ and say when He asks, "Have you anything bothering you?" "No, Lord, how could I have anything bothering me when I am with you?" This is what leads to comprehension of Divine Truth, of the realization of the living Presence of Jesus Christ in our midst. Out of this there should flow a depth of tranquillity, an impenetrable stronghold of serenity of mind to outer senses and the exterior part of the soul, which is in contact with the changing and fickle and unreasonable world of emptiness and the crucifying physical universe, which is simply working out God's rationality and the purifying processes of our souls for eternity.

There should be in our souls one supreme point of peace in the realization that though high winds come, winter or summer, storm or flood, fire or war, nothing shall separate us individually from the peace of God which is in Christ Jesus who is with me, on earth, only a few feet away.[18]

Not many masters of the spiritual life have been as unqualifyingly clear about Christ's human presence on earth in the Eucharist as Father Gerald. What he says about the supreme point of peace from realizing that Jesus is "with me on earth, only a few feet away" is no pious exaggeration. It is the experience of everyone whose faith in the Real Presence has become a living reality.

VI. Relationship to Christ

Christ was the center of everything that Father Gerald wrote or said on the priesthood. Whether exhorting priests to be faithful to their calling, or recalling them to the responsibility they have to the Church of God, the main focus was always on their relationship to Christ. It is His call that leads a man to the altar; it is His grace that sustains him in priestly fidelity; it is His Kingdom that the priest is to labor for and spend himself in saving. In a word, there is only one priesthood, that of Jesus Christ, in which some men are undeservingly privileged to share.

With his characteristic imagery, Father Gerald resorts to many figures of speech to bring out the implications of this relationship, but there are some that are fundamental. Certain attributes of the Savior by which He is known in the New Testament become the key analogies between the chief High Priest and the men whom He ordained to cooperate in His sacerdotal ministry.

LAMB OF GOD

The Sacred Scriptures, and especially the Gospels, are filled with comparisons between the mysteries of faith and things that are known naturally. And always the purpose is to make the mystery either intelligible at all or to bring out its depth of meaning in a way that would be impossible without such comparisons.

Among these analogies, one of the most expressive is the title given to Jesus by John the Baptist when he saw the Savior coming to him. "Look," he said, "there is the Lamb of God that takes away the sin of the world." (John 1:29). The same title, lower case, can be applied to every priest. Why the association? Because of the virtues that Christ wants priests to imitate in following Him, and because of their unique role in the redemption of mankind.

Paradoxical, is it not? The one who has infinite power, yet nevertheless has willed to conquer the souls of men only by His merciful love, by His meekness and by His forbearance.

The lamb is identified in virtue with gentleness, meekness and liturgically with sacrifice, the immolation of self, and so I propose to you as part of our vocation, identification with the Lamb of God.

Every priest is supposed to be identified with Christ who is always not only priest but victim. A priest must aspire not only for the very fulfillment of our priesthood in Christ Jesus, we must not only be offering Him but we must be capable of being offered by Him.[1]

Revelation tells the believer that "only by sacrifice does God remove sin." So only by our sacrifice shall we remove our own sins and those of our fellowmen.

Without sacrifice we are not Christians and without specific sacrifice we shall never accomplish in its wholesomeness the vocation to which God has called us.

What is the essence of sin? The essence of sin is the refusal of the human will to sacrifice itself, even to the Will of God. The little entity, created entity yet immortal, endowed with immortality, knows the Will of God and then deliberately chooses its own will in preference to the Will of God. So the essence of sin is the substitution of one's own will for the Divine Will; and the essence of reparation is conversely, sacrifice of one's own will to the Divine Will. It is said of the Divine Lamb of God that He was "obedient unto death, even to the death of the Cross."[2]

How does this affect a priest? Very intimately. If the essence of reparation for sin is sacrifice, and if priests are to be other Christs, then God asks of them "the immolation of their own wills to the Divine Will."

Among the forms of immolation, "sacrifices that come directly from the Will of God," like ill-health, rejection or "any one of a thousand different afflictions into which one's own will enters only in the acceptance, are preferable in the spiritual life to those that are chosen by our own will."[3]

What, then, is the role of meekness and gentleness in the life of a priest if he is to imitate Christ, the Lamb of God? It is the all-important role of not resisting the Divine Will. After all, what is meekness if not the virtue that moderates anger; and in this case controls the natural tendency of the human will to resent the sometimes hard expectations of a demanding God. And gentleness is simply interior meekness carried into external practice.

It is not strange, therefore, to identify a priest with the Lamb of God because it is perfectly normal to associate the priesthood with sacrifice. But with one important addition. The more willingly a man allows himself to be sanctified, the more fruitful will be his priestly ministry. That is why the laudable ambition of every priest should be that Christ "may echo the words we say to Him; and as we call Him the Lamb of God, so He may in the depths of His Heart smile and say, 'Yes, and this is my lamb, this is my priest who is in me and with me, and by my strength and love is also a lamb for sacrifice.'"[4]

PRECIOUS BLOOD

The model of the Lamb of God as a pattern for priests to imitate was only the first step in an extended comparison between Christ and those whom He ordained for His service. Father Gerald proceeded to build a whole edifice of priestly virtues on this foundation, using St. Peter as his guide. "Remember," the apostle told the first Christians, "the ransom that was paid to free you from the useless way of life your ancestors handed down was not paid in anything corruptible, neither in silver nor gold, but in the precious blood of a Lamb without spot or stain, namely Christ (1 Peter 1:18-19).

But if Christ as the Lamb of God shed His Blood for the salvation of the world, then priests are to shed their blood, according to God's Will, in union with the Savior and in order to apply the fruits of His redemption.

Perhaps no single New Testament term for the redemptive work of Christ appears more often in Father Gerald than "the Precious Blood."

Some twenty years before his death, he wrote a short essay on "The Precious Blood and the Priest" that should be quoted almost in full.

The Precious Blood of Jesus obviously belongs to all men, insomuch as for all men without exception it was poured out on Calvary.

Nevertheless it will be profitable for us priests to reflect upon our special relationship with the Redeeming Blood of Christ.

1. We share with all sinners — aware of what the Blood of Christ has purchased for us — in a debt of gratitude which God's continued patience with us and the forgiveness of our daily transgressions only serves to increase.

2. We share insofar as we have accepted the graces of personal holiness in the gratitude of our Blessed Mother and all the Saints — for all holiness is of the Blood of Jesus. This is made obvious by the grace of our Communions.

3. We share uniquely in Mary's privilege of bringing the Precious Blood to men. Her Immaculate Heart is the fountainhead but for the continued presence of the Blood of Jesus upon our altars God deigns to utilize us, His priests, so that effectively we share in Mary's privilege of giving the Blood of Jesus to the world.

4. We administer the fruits of the Precious Blood every time we administer the Holy Sacraments and most specifically in every sacramental absolution.

These reflections tend to make the thoughtful priest anxious to deepen his gratitude and devotion to the Precious Blood, to quicken his desire to offer the Chalice of Salvation with greater tenderness, reverence, and humility, and to resolve to glorify the Blood of Jesus by lifelong fidelity to that priestly self-discipline of which the Blood of Jesus is both the source, inspiration and everlasting reward.

"May the Blood of Jesus quicken us to the glory of God and the salvation of immortal souls."[5] On the theme of the Precious Blood is woven practically every feature of the priesthood, especially the responsibility it imposes on the ordained to be worthy witnesses of the Savior, who is now saving souls through their sacramental ministry.

"How I rejoice with you," Father Gerald writes to a fellow priest who is being sorely tried in his labors, "Jesus loves you. He proves it by giving you, by sharing with you, His own, His very own priesthood. How can you ever repay Him?" The answer is by uniting your trials with those of the Savior.

O my Brother, do not drink the Chalice of the Lord only at the visible altar, but let your soul be His temple, your heart His invisible altar, and there drink the mystical chalice of our Lord's sufferings, sacrifices, humiliations, disappointments. If you only pray, pray perseveringly to His Spirit and to His Mother, all will go well.

I shall pray for you always, and you must do the same for me. God has given me, these many years, the grace to recognize that neither race nor color counts with Him and consequently should not count with us; we are brothers — we who share His Priesthood, we who have Christ as an Eldest Brother and His Blood as the Sacred Bond of our amity.[6]

He opens a letter to a young man about to be ordained, with the greeting, "with what joy I write you this letter in the Blood of Jesus. I can almost feel the Precious Blood falling on my hands as I write, for am I not a priest, and am I not writing to one who is so soon to be a priest and hold the Precious Blood lovingly aloft before the eyes of the world in the chalice of his virgin soul!"

So you are to be a chalice, my Brother, a chalice for Christ, with Christ, in Christ, and you will find it sweet, I am sure, for you will be generous.

When a priest is generous with God, or even tries to be, he is bound to be happy. This truth holds true in all vocations but perhaps in no vocation so assuredly as in that of the Priesthood, for when a priest tries to be generous, he is dealing directly with God and God is divinely generous.

Be, therefore, dear Brother, generous with Christ; ask Him to make of your soul a Roman chalice, with the broad, heavy base of humility, the straight stem of singleness of purpose, and the ample, wide cup of generosity. Ask His Holy Spirit, as well, to adorn it with the virtues — gems that shall delight both God and His angels. And as for me, I shall daily ask our Blessed Mother to keep your chalice and mine and the souls of all priests, our brothers in Christ, chaste and holy and thus less unworthy of the lips and the Blood of Jesus Christ.[7]

Still again, he writes to a priest to remind him that this is precisely what the priesthood means, a lifetime sharing in the Passion of Christ. But the strength to live this life is always there, in the Precious Blood which the priest is both to consecrate and, by consuming, imitate for the upbuilding of Christ's Body which is the Church.

In a true priest, God has given, man has given — the result is a work of Love, Divine and human. The priesthood offers man the supremest way of giving all to God. This is what Our Lord meant when, turning to those same sons of Zebedee, He asked them quietly, "Can you drink of My Chalice?"

That is what the priesthood really means, a chance to drink of the Chalice of our Lord, a chance to add your life and blood to His life and Blood; a chance to lift His Chalice to your lips and the chalice of your soul to His lips; a chance to give till there is nothing left to give — till the arms of death receive you from the arms of the cross and IN you to the arms of Jesus and His Mother Mary.[8]

Finally, in a letter to his ordination class, on their anniversary of receiving the priesthood, Father Gerald goes back in memory over the years that have slipped between. "We are still young, are we not, still newly ordained? I hope so, still with our first fervor and zeal and innocence, preserved for us by the Blood of Christ!"

It is this Blood of Christ, which they daily bring down on the altar, that unites priests in a blood relationship of grace that has no human counterpart.

How closely one in spirit should we be — we priests — seeing that morning by morning the same Blood purples our lips, crimsons our hearts, purifies our souls. Why should we not be one in heart, and mind and soul, we priests of Jesus, nourished by the Blood of His Own Heart. Why should we not be joyous, we who have such a daily pledge of His undying love. Why should we not be holy, we who are inebriated with the Life Blood of God's Holy One. "I know Thee, who Thou art," cried out the evil spirit. "Thou Holy One of God!" Every priest should be able to win like recognition from the foes of God and Holy Church. There is a mysterious force in real holiness; it can win recognition even from the devil, not to say from men.

But I am wandering. What I want to ask is this: Have you ever felt, after the Communion of the Precious Blood, a sense of humility, born of the realization of the greatness of His giving and the littleness of ours? O, if ever God, who is Generosity Divine, has been generous, it is with us, His priests, He has been generous. Others, Christ has made His children. Of us — He has made Himself.

With feeble recognition and thin gratitude we answer all this largesse of Almighty God. Like James and John, He has invited us to drink of His Chalice — we have and shall do so faithfully day by day. It has all been very sweet thus far, and I trust we shall grow stronger so that we may drink the dregs of bitterness and trial as unhesitatingly as we have supped of the depths of devotion and consolation. Are you prepared for this? We priests must be preparing for Gethsemane even while we dwell on Tabor. When we shall have emptied Life's chalice — we shall be given another brimming one — overflowing with eternal joy.[9]

Given this penetrating grasp of the mission of a priest, sent into the world to help redeem the world by his life of sacrifice, it was only natural that Father Gerald should name the community of Sisters he founded Handmaids of the Precious Blood. They were to be just that, servants of the Savior who shed His Blood to reconcile sinners with the Father. But their mission was to be very specific, to sacrifice their lives for priests, the faithful ones so they might remain loyal to the Master, and for those who had strayed so they might return to the one who ordained them.

"The great mistake," the Handmaids were told, "of the priests who fail God is that they forget that the priest must also be the victim." Someone, then, must pray and make reparation where priests have failed to do so. The Handmaids, therefore, and the faithful they inspire to join them, must "identify yourselves with the Precious Blood by a willingness to suffer, not in some way you choose, but in the way *He* chooses. A victim does not choose his own form of immolation; that is for the one making the sacrifice, that is for your Divine Lover to choose."

And what is the value of this kind of immolation, "what becomes of this sacrifice?" Those for whom it is offered, in the spirit of faith, are immensely benefited by God's grace. "The priest who not only is priest but victim immediately becomes powerful in Christ to do what Christ has done. What is that? Raise souls to life again in the Sacrament of Penance, and the priest becomes another Christ, saying to a soul, 'Lazarus, come forth.'"[10]

In this vision of the priesthood, priests need the faithful to join with them in sacrifice for the continued saving work of the Precious Blood of Christ.

THE BRIDEGROOM

The very idea of cooperating with Christ requires an intimacy with Christ on which the priest must presume. Otherwise what he expects Our Lord to do through him would be folly, if not blasphemy. There must be a nearness to the Son of God that is logically prior to a priest's claim to being an instrument of God's grace.

Father Gerald identified this nearness with the title by which the Savior more than once called Himself: namely, the Bridegroom. There is, of course, a prior and universal sense in which Christ is the Bridegroom of every soul that believes in Him, and the writings of the mystics abound in rich imagery of supernatural espousal between Christ and the devoted faithful who love Him.

Then, building on the teaching of many Fathers of the Church, Father Gerald saw in the miracle at the marriage feast at Cana a perfect symbol of the Incarnation, which is the fundamental marvel of Christianity. In this miracle of miracles, "the Son of God was wedding human nature. He was taking human nature unto Himself by the hypostatic union, and in the virginal womb of His Mother, He was wedding humanity."[11]

But if all of this is true of people in general, and of those who are Christians, it is more than ever true of those whom Christ has ordained to the priesthood. "Especially and immediately, we must say, Christ was wedding humanity in the souls and bodies of those who would be privileged, day by day as we are, His priests to bend over a little white host and identify it with ourselves." This calls for some explanation.

> A priest is wedded to Christ. Our parents were wedded to Christ and in Christ that in their oneness of living in God they should continue the work of creation. You and I, dear Fathers, are wedded to Christ not for a sexual purpose, but for a purpose of intimate union that has in mind the redemption of mankind and our union is superior to the sacrament of matrimony because in matrimony it is two creatures, there are two created lovers who are united in one uncreated love and lovers. But in our union with Christ there is no other created being concerned in the oneness itself; a Divine person takes the place of a human person, a Divine person who utilizes all our powers of body and soul for the accomplishment and continuation and especially for the fulfillment of the unloosening of the great channels of salvation, the reservoir of salvation that He established in His Passion. And that He releases to the world only through our passion, only through our passion.[12]

The implications of this fact are startling, but also predictable. If a priest is to become as fruitful in the salvation of souls as Christ wants him to be, he has no choice. He must join sacrifice with sacrifice, his own with that of the Redeemer. And among the sacrifices that a priest must make, his lifelong celibacy has special efficacy in rearing a supernatural offspring for God.

He cannot be a fruitful partner to Christ except by abiding in Christ and giving Christ that sovereignty of love that belongs in the — matrimony to — mutually one partner to another. We are like the Blessed Mother fruitful to God — wedded to God in virginity and fruitful to God in absolute chastity, as she brought forth, without the sacrifice or the impairment of her virginity, her absolute immaculate virginity. So the priest brings forth Christ at the altar day by day and the more like the Blessed Mother he is in his virginal heart and chaste and disciplined body so much the more joyously does the Son of God rest in his arms.[13]

There is an implicit covenant in all of this, between the priest and Christ. Absolutely speaking, because he has the power of orders, a priest can validly consecrate and validly absolve no matter what his state of soul may be. And the Church has more than once condemned the error of those who would identify a priest's ability to exercise his sacramental powers with the sanctity of his personal life.

But there is more here than just a re-affirmation of the sacrament of orders, which, as a sacrament, has the built-in ability to confer the grace it signifies. What Father Gerald is arguing for is the terrible need for sanctity in priests. Otherwise, they will have the power to confer the sacraments but people may not be ready to accept their priestly ministrations and God will not use them to the limit of their capacity as channels of His saving mercy. This applies with special poignancy to the people's use of the sacrament of penance. And it points up the significance of what Pope John Paul II told the American Bishops on his pilgrimage to America. "In the face of a widespread phenomenon of our time," said the Pope, "namely, that many of our people, who are among the great numbers who receive Communion, make little use of confession, we must emphasize Christ's basic call to conversion. We must also stress that the personal encounter with the forgiving Jesus in the sacrament of reconciliation is a divine means which keeps alive in our heads and our communities, a consciousness of sin in its perennial and tragic reality, and which actually brings forth, by the action of Jesus and the power of His Spirit, fruits of conversion in justice and holiness of life."[14]

Father Gerald would say that one conclusion to be drawn from this is the need for greater holiness in priests. They must be personally nearer in spirit to the Bridegroom of their souls.

On the one hand, priests are gifted with divine powers for healing sinners that have been the scandal of unbelievers.

You can go as far as you like as long as you go with reverence and meekness and humility in thinking of the identity of a priest with Christ. He shares with us according as we are willing to have Him share with us, as far as we are interested in Him, in proportion as He is the dominant love of our souls, He shares with us His own ineffable life. He will forgive sin through us the great barrier between souls and the Kingdom of heaven. Who can forgive sin, they said, when He started to exercise His magnificent mercy of God — who can forgive sin but God? Which after all, is theologically and philosophically true, but Christ was God, and when we forgive sin as His delegates, it is He who forgives. Christ is in us, is in the faithful priest reconciling the world to His Father. How wonderful! And how wonderful our vocation! "For Christ," St. Paul says, "we are ambassadors." We're more than ambassadors. Oftentimes an ambassador must communicate back by radio or in one way or another — cable — with the one who is greater than he, the one who has sent him, the President or the Minister or the Chancellor or the Secretary of State to whom he is immediately responsible. We don't need to do that. Christ liveth in us, the Divine Supreme King of Kings. We are His ambassadors but we are also identified with the King much more fully than any ambassador. He ratifies our works, He ratifies our decisions: 'Whatsoever thou shalt loose on earth, shall be loosed in heaven; whatsoever thou shalt bind on earth, shall be bound also in heaven." That's more than an ambassador can do.

The contracts that we make are signed by us and as we sign them, Christ signs them with the Blood of His Heart, He writes the receipt in full for our absolutions. O how marvelous is the life of a priest! It is Jesus Christ finding another way to live on in the world and to go about doing good.[15]

Since the priesthood is so powerful to reconcile sinners with God, and draw them away from evil, the devil is most eager to draw priests away from sanctity. He knows he cannot deprive a priest of his sacerdotal power to remove sin, but if he succeeds in seducing a priest from nearness to Christ, he has weakened the priest's influence with the people. The evil spirit is very shrewd.

> Just because a priest can be and ought to be, and he lives according to his conscience and to the grace of his apostolate, as Christ in the world, just because this is true, he is the particular object of the malice of the devil. The evil spirit — the forces of evil — would rather eliminate one priest than a thousand laymen. They would rather bring one priest to disgrace than a thousand laymen. It is more advantageous to the interests of evil.[16]

No wonder priests can say, "How precious is our vocation in the sight of God. How terrible is our vocation in the sight of demons. Because this is true, you must be vigilant in guarding your own immortal souls." If as great a priest as St. Paul could beg the Christians of his day, "Pray for me, lest having preached to others, I myself become a castaway," how much more should others who are less holy than Paul ask the faithful, that as priests they remain faithful to the great privilege of saving souls.

Perhaps nowhere else did Father Gerald show himself more prophetic than what he foresaw would take place before the end of the twentieth century: a massive and successful propaganda against the existence of sin. With the notion of sin removed or obscured, it is easy to reduce the priesthood to an archaic form of piety that has no particular value in modern society.

> One of the most important things that we must emphasize in our own lives is what the devil in the twentieth century is very cleverly trying to soften, trying to make men forget. It is quite simple because the mercy of God is over all His work, because modern science investigating the hu-

manity of man, the corporeal nature of man finds so many
things that lessen — that tend to lessen — so many pres-
sures and areas of pressure upon his soul that they can
find subtle excuses for the aberrations of the human soul.
Even in Catholic theology, and I make this as a prophecy,
there will come a time when the Holy Father will have to
speak out against the infiltration of philosophical and kin-
dred ideas that tend to lessen the responsibility of man for
his actions.

It was necessary for our Lord to speak of the Holy Spirit
as convincing the world of sin. Chesterton has told us that
one of the great sins, one of the basic sins of our age, was
the denial of sin.[17]

The logic of the evil spirit is perfect. He knows that, as the
reality of sin becomes less clear, the people's sense of guilt is weakened and gradually disappears. What is the purpose of confession, or
the sacrament of penance or, for that matter, of a priesthood that al-
legedly was instituted by Christ to remit sin and restore sinners to
friendship with God? Forgiveness implies the existence of sin that
needs to be forgiven. But if practically no one commits mortal sins
anymore, what is the meaning of the sacrament of reconciliation,
except as the relic of a former, theologically unenlightened age?

Father Gerald could be outspoken, when the occasion called
for righteous indignation. That is why he warned priests of the erro-
neous ideas that were looming over the horizon.

You make a mockery of the Cross, dear Fathers, you make
a mockery of our religion, you make a mockery of the
daily Mass, if there is not such a thing as sin and hell. The
life of our Lord becomes — as it is in reality, not becomes,
as it is in reality — a road-block cast up by Divine mercy,
to try to stop millions from casting themselves into hell.
God was not bluffing when He permitted His Divine Son
to be nailed to a cross.[18]

Consequently, remaining faithful to Christ means remaining
docile to His teachings. And among these teachings none is more
crucial than the Savior's doctrine on sin. We commonly associate a

temptation of the devil with being seduced to indulge in unlawful pleasures. But the devil is also, and principally, a deceiver. He tries to make us believe that what is, in fact, a lie is actually the truth.

In this critical area, on which the whole structure of Christianity depends, everyone must ask for light not to be deceived. "The Eternal Word, without whom the Father does nothing that He does, was not bluffing, was not making merely a gesture, when He whispered in the agony in the Garden, 'Pray that you fall not into temptation.' No one is excluded from this necessity to ask for divine assistance." Certainly, "priests. . . and bishops are not exempted." Indeed, "all of us must turn to this Divine Bridegroom" in constant prayer so as not to be deceived by the evil spirit.[19]

THE WAY

There is one more relationship to Christ that Father Gerald urges priests to foster, namely, as the Way.

True enough, when the Savior said He was the Way, He meant that for all mankind He is the unique path to the Father, and the only road that anyone who wants to be saved must follow. But the same title has a distinctive meaning for priests. "The Incarnate Word comes to every priest not only out of personal love but He also says to that priest, 'Clothe me with your flesh, clothe me with your blood, give me your lips that I may speak, for I am the Truth.'"[20]

In other words, Christ is the Way not only as the channel of mercy and pattern of sanctity for the priest himself, but also the Way by which He uses the priest to serve as vehicle of grace and model of holiness for others. In effect, Christ tells the priest: "Give me your heart that I may love mankind, give me your eyes that I may look out with compassion on the multitudes, give me your mind that I may flood it with the love of faith, give me your feet that they may take me on sick calls, that I may go to the sick and dying, that I may go to the fallen nations that sit in darkness."[21]

The Savior asks the priest to leave all things; to become another Christ; to leave his own mother in imitation of Christ. And above all, "to leave his one little ugly ego, to die to himself and allow Christ to live within him."

He asks for everything a priest has. And that is why our vocation is so sublime and also so difficult for human nature. We must be totally capitulated to Christ. Think of the magnificent truth contained in those words of St. Paul: "I live, no not I, but Christ liveth in me." The Holy Spirit compelled him to say those words. The Son of God dominated Paul and the Son of God wants to dominate us. So you see there is for us a *sursum corda,* an Ascension required even on earth: We must ascend out of our nothingness, we must ascend into the Heart and Mind of Christ, so that we have no mind but Christ's, no heart but Christ's Heart, no hands but Christ's Hands. That's what it means: "I am dead," again as St. Paul, "I am dead, and my life is hidden with Christ in God." So the individual priest, like Mary, is the object of love of the whole adorable Trinity. We must surrender to Christ, we must belong to Him.[22]

What are the consequences of such total surrender? Men of this caliber become potent instruments of divine blessing. "When we belong to Him, He uses us as a *Via,* we become part of the Way. A good priest is the highway of salvation for thousands of souls." Take the case of St. John Vianney.

To the Cure of Ars, God forced the evil spirit to say: "You have taken eighty thousand souls away from me." Isn't that magnificent? Even apart from that, think of the priests who went to confession to him and who went back to their parishes, to their religious communities, the Bishops who went back to their dioceses with a new life and who themselves spread the flame that had been rekindled at the hearth of this parish priest. See what is given to us in our vocation.[23]

Such is the high calling, and also the grave responsibility, of every priest. The Master wants to use him as the way that leads others to heaven and sanctification. And he will be as effective in the hands of Christ as he is united with the Heart of Christ. This is the verdict of, by now, nineteen centuries of the Church's history.

VII. Living the Mass

Given his exalted understanding of the priesthood, whose central purpose is to offer the Sacrifice of the Mass, it was inevitable that Father Gerald would urge priests to live the Mass which they celebrated.

The priest, he insisted, "has to be the image of Jesus Christ." But, then, who or what is Jesus Christ? He is two things. He is priest and victim. He is the one who offers and the one who is offered.

What, therefore, Christ is mystically, the earthly priest is to be correspondingly in the Mass. Like his Master, he is not "content alone to be a priest at the altar, but he wants to be also the Host at the altar. He wants not only to be Christ's priest bright in the beautiful vestments of the Mass — the formal vestments of the liturgical service — but he also wants beneath to be crucified. He wants to be one with the Crucified. He wants to be a Host."[1]

NOT ONLY PRIEST BUT VICTIM

Among the rubrics to be observed by the priest at the altar, none is more demanding than the "inmost rubric," the spiritual rubric of sacrifice. "I must, as a priest, not only be a *sacerdos* but I must be a *hostia.*" Strange as the term may sound, "we have to be hosted with Christ."

For all priests, and not only for religious, this sacrifice is to be modeled on the sacrifice that Christ reveals in the Mass.

It is first of all a sacrifice of obedience. "We lift Christ to the Father every morning and His sacrifice is complete. His immolation in the little white Host and in the unique species of the wine is a complete immolation. Is He not completely in our hands, obeying us His creatures? Do we obey the God, our God," who is so obedient to us?[2]

It is, moreover, a sacrifice of poverty. "Could anything be poorer than the little white Host?" No wonder the Savior in the species "moves with ease." He is "detached from everything." No wonder, "without an effort, indeed lovingly," Christ in the Host "leaves the ciborium to go into the heart of the poorest little man or woman, priest or religious who comes to Him, who leaves the golden ciborium with zeal, with anxious love to hide in the heart of some dying sinner."[3] The embarrassing question for priests is, "Are we in that way to Christ in all things?" In other words, are priests thus poor in spirit? "Be detached," they are told, "even from such little comforts as men easily get attached to. Our poor little hearts are like little bits of ivy that are poking out tendrils and clinging even to stones: men become attached to almost anything and this attachment is terribly delaying to the soul in its movements towards God. Men can get attached even to poverty — to a broken picture or a broken bed. Be attached to nothing except God."[4] Only by cultivating total detachment from creatures will a priest become another Christ to the people he is meant to serve.

The final sacrifice of Christ in the Mass, which the priest is called upon to imitate, is the purity of selfless love. It was out of love, and love alone, that Christ died on the Cross. And it is in the Mass that He continues to manifest this love. That is why "Jesus in the Blessed Sacrament is the very source of our purity, the source of our strength." He is this source twice over: once by the example of chastity as selfless charity, which Christ gives us in the Holy Sacrifice; and once again by the graces He confers through the Eucharistic Liturgy to make possible the practice of chastity.

> We are offered in exchange for the renunciation of human love and human consolation, we are offered not angelic love, we are offered Divine Love. We are offered the ultimate love of the human entity. Any human rational relation that is to attain to happiness, is going to attain to happiness in God. In God and in God alone. Now all these things are ours in the Mass.[5]

REVELATION OF LOVE

Father Gerald saw the Mass as a sacrifice and a sacrament. It is a sacrifice because it re-enacts now what the Savior did when He died on Calvary, only the manner of offering, on Christ's part, is no longer bloody. He is now glorified and can no longer die. But we are still mortal, beginning with the priest at the altar and extending to all the members of Christ's Mystical Body on earth. We are therefore able to shed blood, as we are expected to, either in body if that be God's will, or at least in spirit, which is always His will: to surrender ourselves to His demands and die to ourselves in doing what He wants.

Furthermore, the Mass is a sacrament because it obtains for all believers, and especially for the priest, the graces needed to live up to the Savior's expectations of His followers. Indeed, the Mass is the principal source of power we have to remain faithful to the Gospel.

But this is not all. Besides being a sacrifice and sacrament, the Mass is a revelation of love. Father Gerald proposed this idea somewhat cautiously, fearful that he might be saying more than he should. But he need not have been afraid. His insight is fully in agreement with the Church's teaching, and it offers the priest a deeper understanding of his dignity.

"What is the essential story of the Mass?" he asks. It is bound up with the mystery of the Trinity. When, at the Last Supper Christ ordained the Apostles and told them, "Do this in memory of Me," was He referring only to Himself "the man of sorrows, the Son of God who is entering into His Passion"? If so, then "the Holy Sacrifice is thought of, correctly and exactly, as the Memorial of the Passion of Our Lord. As St. Paul says in his treatment of it: You shall show forth the death of the Lord until He comes."

But can this ME of the Last Supper refer to something more, and not only (though also) to the Passion of Christ in time? Yes, reasons Father Gerald. It can likewise refer to the divine life of love shared by the Three Persons in the Godhead.

If you turn to the actual naked text, Our Lord said: Do this in memory of ME, and the ME is first of all the Eternal Word. From this I argue that the Mass should be, and is, not only a drama of the suffering life of Our Lord but a drama of the Eternal Life of the Word. The life that the Word lives in the bosom of the Father from eternity to eternity. And so I ask myself: What is that life? Insofar as humbly we are permitted to look upon the life of the Adorable Trinity of God, how is that life revealed to men? St. Augustine represents God the Father as being Eternal Love: it is a love that gives — a loving love. LOVE LOVING equals God the Father. LOVE LOVED equals God the Son. The LOVE of the LOVING LOVE is God the Holy Ghost.

So the life of the Blessed Trinity within the Trinity is a life of mutual love.[6]

What, then, does the priest do at Mass? By his words of consecration, he makes present on the altar the Second Person of the Trinity become man. When he elevates the Host and Chalice, he is elevating the Son of God "and offers Him back to the Father."

As a little child might lift something precious that has been given to him, and then as the parent reached to take it, draws it back to himself: so in a very beautiful movement we offer — indeed the prayer that follows the consecration indicates that — that our gift be taken by the hands of angels and borne to the Father. But no angel takes the Host away from the paten, no angel draws up the Precious Blood, tubes it up out of our chalice. We offer it to God but we retain it, we bring it back, we hold it. We are like the spouse in the words of the Canticle of Canticles: we hold the Divine Lover and we will not let Him go. We need Him. He is always with the Father making intercession for us. And we need Him here on earth. And where does He terminate? Where do the Father and the Son terminate and consummate their love in the Eucharist? In the souls of the priest and the communicants who are the Mystical Body of Christ, the Temples of the Holy Ghost.[7]

In the light of these insights, how are we to finally describe the Mass? It is a continuous revelation of God's love, not only His love for sinful mankind, but His love within Himself, as the Triune God.

In the sacrifice of the Mass, Christ's ordained priests "bring forth the Eternal Word. We give Him to the Father and we terminate His union with the Father in our souls and in the souls of the communicants who are the Temples of the Holy Ghost."

Implied in this view of the Mass is a view of the Incarnation that specially appealed to Father Gerald. He knew, of course, that God became man to restore a fallen mankind to divine friendship. But he also believed that God would have become man even though man had never sinned, just to show how much He loves us. Taught by such eminent saints as Francis de Sales, this opinion lends itself to many attractive conclusions.

We may, therefore, look upon the Mass as a daily invitation to imitate the selfless love of the Trinity, made manifest in the Eucharistic Liturgy. "Every Christian must live that but especially a priest who is under the urgent necessity of living the life of Christ." And, "what is the life of Christ? The Eternal Word. He receives all from the Father and He gives back to the Father within the encompassing of the Holy Spirit."

Once a priest realizes this awesome fact, however dimly, he is moved to pray and ask the Lord whom he brings down on the altar at Mass to inspire him with some semblance of the same charity.

Lord Jesus, give us the grace so to live to take all with Thee and in Thee from the Father. To take all; to take the successes and the failures: the sunshiny days and the cold raw days: the contradictions, the limitations, the frailties of life: to take them all as so many little grains of wheat and to crush them in the Mill of Your Divine Love, with the pressure of the Divine Love, to make of it beautiful little Hosts. To take all and give all within the encompassing wings of the Holy Ghost.

Lord Jesus, make us Thy priests, all priests, a mystical heart for Thyself, a healthy heart that takes your beautiful throbbing warm and pure blood and takes it into our own being; and then our hearts throbbing with your love and your love throbbing in our hearts send that blood forth through the arteries and veins of the Mystical Body until the whole world — the children of men — shall all be living members of the One and Eternal Word, the Word made flesh, the High Priest who has honored us with an absorption into His priesthood.

And do thou, O Blessed Mother, Queen of the clergy, pray for us that we may humbly and in some little way begin to comprehend the greatness of the love with which we are comprehended.[8]

Since God is love, as St. John tells us, and God became man; then love became incarnate in the Person of Jesus Christ. And this Jesus Christ becomes present daily in the Mass through the power of His priests. More than anyone else, they are obligated to pattern their lives on the Savior who ordained them.

THE TWO TRANSUBSTANTIATIONS

Father Gerald had no difficulty associating the miracle of the Incarnation with the miracle of Transubstantiation. Speaking of the words of consecration (in Latin, *Hoc est enim corpus meum),* he described them as "five Latin words that unite heaven and earth, God and man, and man and God, in an embrace of actual oneness. The only words comparable are the words our Blessed Mother spoke when she was invited to give her consent to the Incarnation: 'Be it done to me according to thy word.'"

Taking his cue from certain early Fathers of the Church when they wrote about the Mass, Father Gerald compares the alliance created when God first became man with the alliance He seeks to create through the Sacrifice of the Mass.

When the Son of God leapt as it were from the bosom of the Father into the bosom of the little Jewish maiden whom He had kept immaculate in her conception, there was an alliance being set up. God was undertaking directly and immediately in Person to correct the folly of mankind. And when God comes to us in Holy Communion and when, as priests, God comes to our hands in the consecration, He is intent not only from the application of redemption, not only continuing the ineffable glory of His Father, but He is also intent upon our immediate salvation.

He comes with a very great personal intent to His priests. He comes to make Himself one with us and to make us one with Him: He comes to transubstantiate us.[9]

Carrying the comparison one step further, priests are reminded of Adam's statement when Eve was made from the side of Adam. When she was brought to him, Adam said: "This is flesh of my flesh; this is bone of my bone." A priest can apply these words to himself.

Equivalently he said: This is my body. And for this cause shall a man leave his mother and father and shall cleave to his wife and they shall be two in one flesh. And now of course we must have sublime minds and a priest ought to cultivate a sublime mind all the days of his life. But when we sublimate this which is the natural law, a marvelous application can be made to the relationship of Christ and His priests. For after all, it is for the sake of Christ, for our personal love for Christ and for the privilege of saying Mass and holding His Body and Blood, Soul and Divinity in our hands, of His belonging to us and our belonging to Him; that we have left mother and father and we cleave to our dear Divine Lord in a virginal union but in a union that is even more intimate than the consummation of marriage. The Son of God, the Infinite, All-holy, All-wise, Almighty God has willed to become one with us and has willed us to say what even the angels cannot say: This is My Body. This is My Blood.

How deeply, how tenderly a priest should whisper those words all the days of his life. His lips have become the lips of God, and Nature exercises its obediential faculty: it yields the silent elements of bread and wine, yields their substance at our command and lo we become like Mary, holding, on Christmas Eve, her God as a tiny little help-less Babe. If a priest could once see the glory of the Incarnate Word, it would be with great difficulty that he would have the power to say those words: he would probably faint before the glory and the beauty of God, he would swoon with the tenderness, with the love light, in the eyes of Christ upon him: This is My Body. If he is living in fidelity to his priestly discipline, these words are recognized by Christ in the equivalent of an Amen.

The Pope at Rome, the Vicar of Christ, has no more sublime power, no more direct contact with Divinity than the simplest, newly-ordained priest who whispers those words. The important thing for a priest is that he will say these words with increasing love and devotion. They speak of a priest's "first fervor." I pray that the Spirit will give you all devotion, and pray to the Holy Ghost that your devotion to the Mass will increase, and increase, and increase until the last day of your life, and that your last Mass may be your most fervent Mass.

How blessed would be the priest who would make that his philosophy of life: to so live that his Mass each morning would be more completely an expression of, not only God's sublime love for him, but of his sublime immolation to God. When Our Lord speaks through our lips and changes the bread into His living flesh, He has accomplished both an object and a means: the means is the glory of God, first through the offering of Himself as an immolation to His Father, and then, by the communication of His Body and Blood, His Mystical Body the Church and especially His priests might progressively be transubstantiated into Him. He wants to be immolated, He wants to be offered in another way, He wants to be offered in us. He wants to be able to say over us, as we say over Him: This is My Body.[10]

Both transubstantiations are part of the Church's understanding of the priesthood. But they differ immensely in their efficacy. Christ never fails to become physically present in the Mass, whenever the priest pronounces the words of consecration. Jesus is always responsive to His priest. But the priest must want to cooperate with the graces he receives from the Eucharist, in order to be transformed supernaturally into Christ. Yet the first transubstantiation is a condition for the second. It is mainly through the power of the Mass and Holy Communion that the priest — and then the faithful — become partakers of Christ's divinity who for love of us became partaker of our humanity.

VIII. The Priest and Mary

There is one fundamental reason why a priest should be especially devoted to the Blessed Virgin Mary. He is ordained to bring the living Christ on earth in the Holy Sacrifice, to make the living Christ available to the faithful in Holy Communion, and to keep the living Christ on earth in the Blessed Sacrament. In his own way, therefore, a priest continues the miracle of the Incarnation that Mary first made possible at Nazareth and Bethlehem. If, as St. Augustine so beautifully expresses it, *Caro Jesu, Caro Mariae,* the flesh of Jesus is the flesh of Mary, then a priest who has the power of consecrating the Body and Blood of Christ should be most devoted — after his love of Christ — to the Mother who brought Christ into the world and therefore made the Eucharist a present Reality.

GRACE BUILDS ON NATURE

But as we look more closely, there are other reasons, too, why we should expect priests to be particularly devoted, we might almost say attached, to the Mother of Christ. "A man is always a child to his own mother," Father Gerald observed, "always a little one, always in need of his mother." And the need is commonly reciprocated. Mothers never forget that their sons somehow depend on them and the sons, if they remain normal, always retain a wholesome sense of the need of a mother's solicitude and care. Father Gerald recalled "following the wake of the last war, the army chaplains found out more often than not, that when a soldier was going to die it was not even his wife he would ask for; he would revert to his childhood and would want his mother."[1]

There is a deep-grained relationship in a man's heart with his mother that is a law of nature. And the greater his sense of gratitude to the woman who gave him birth, the deeper and more lasting his affection for her, in spite of the passage of time or the entrance into his life of other persons who also claim his devotion and love.

Grace elevates this law of nature, and further refines it in a priest whose vocation calls for a life of celibacy. Then, if a man is honestly conscious within himself of past, and grave, infidelities, he has all the more reason, based on faith, to rely on the Blessed Virgin as his mother in the spirit. "There is a time," we can say, "when man can so offend the race that everyone but his mother will desert him. His brothers and sisters and perhaps even his father will disown him. But normally his mother, whose flesh and blood he is, will not disown him but will cling to him to the last."[2]

While these insights apply to every priest, they are especially pertinent to those whose priestly life has been shoddy and who, since ordination, may have strayed far from the practice of even elementary Christian virtue. Men like this desperately need to know that, no matter how far they may have wandered from God, the Mother of God cares for them still. Their inspiration comes from the scene that took place when the dead Christ was taken down from the cross and laid in the arms of His Mother.

Faith tells us that a person in mortal sin is supernaturally dead. And if the person is a priest, he may be compared to the dead Christ, "for the charity of Christ is not in him."

> How tenderly the Mother of God bends over the souls of Christians who are in mortal sin. How steadily upon those lifeless bodies, those cold bodies, fall her tears, seeking to wash them. How warmly and tightly she holds that body seeking to warm it again into life, as the prophet, in symbolism of Christ, warmed the dead son of the Shunammite into life again (cf. 2 Kings 4:32-37). So our Blessed Mother, the mother of all mothers, bends over the souls in the Church that are the living image of her dead Son, and works and labors and prays unceasingly, making, with Her Divine Son, unceasing representation before the throne of God: that Her firstborn Son might not have died in vain for these other Christs.[3]

Mary, we might say, is the priest's final refuge of mercy, and the priest knows it almost instinctively, from his understanding of how enduring is a mother's love for her sons.

A MARIAN LIFE

What Father Gerald recommended to priests was more than ordinary devotion to the Blessed Virgin. He did not hesitate to tell them, "We must live our whole life with our Blessed Mother, without tiring, without any weakening of our resolution." Specifically, "we must be contented to stand and to labor, to weep and to pray and to immolate, with Mary at the foot of the cross."[4] Why should a priest's devotion focus on the Sorrowful Mother, and even more immediately on Her role as the Stabat Mater under the Cross? Because his role as priest is mainly to continue Christ's mission of reconciling sinners with an offended God; and Mary shared in that mission in a unique way all Her life but especially on Calvary.

It can be said with security that God gives His Mother "in a particular way to His priests." And while the beloved disciple beneath the Cross represented all believers, "St. John" was specially "the representative of the priesthood," when he received "in a formal statement and donation the sublime gift of the Mother of God to be his mother."

> In the Garden of Paradise, God had said to Satan: I will put enmity between thee and the woman. Here was the woman at the foot of the Cross. O Lord, the same enmity that God has placed between Thy Mother Immaculate and Satan as symbolic of all invasion of the Will of God, we beg Thee to place in our hearts: we who are the Servants of Her Immaculate Spouse and in Thee Her very sons.[5]

If priests are par excellence Mary's sons in the spirit, it is only to be expected that they should act accordingly. But saying this is only the beginning. It will take constant effort and earnest prayer to acquire the disposition of living united with Christ but in the company of Mary. Hence the following petition to Mary's Son.

> O Jesus, give us the deep and perfect faith that makes a priest live under the bright burden of Our Lady's eyes and under the warm radiance of Thy most beautiful face and

most loving Heart. Make us glad with the gladsomeness of faith, when like Peter and John we are found worthy to suffer something for the sake of the Lord Jesus. Make us rejoice as Thy Heart rejoices and rejoiced in every honor given to Thy Blessed Mother. Make us resolve that our whole life will be Marian as Thy life from its first beginning on earth till the dawn of eternity will be a Marian existence. Under the shadows of Thy Mother's Immaculate Heart Thou didst begin Thy life on earth: with Thy Mother at Thy side Thou art living in eternity. The eyes of Thy Blessed Mother are upon Thee and upon us.

O Jesus grant us the graces so to live day by day that we may not be afraid to lift our eyes in life or in death to meet the face of Mary. O do we not know that by faith, that if we shall see Our Blessed Mother smiling a welcome to us when we die, in that one smile a lifetime of renunciation, of self-conquest, of self-discipline will seem as a great nothingness, a great brevity? The beginning of eternity — the smile of Mary upon the soul of a priest as the Angel of death presents it at the judgment of God.[6]

A concluding exhortation to priests, reminding them that "someone has tried to inspire men with the saying 'The eyes of the world are upon you.'" How much more inspiring to be told that "the eyes of the Mother of God are upon us and we must not fail her. We will not fail her tomorrow, unless we fail her today. We will not fail her today if we remember that the sweetest privilege of a priest is to be worthy of the love of Jesus Christ and the smile of the eyes of Mary."[7] Those who have lived under this inspiration know how effective it is in maintaining one's own priestly integrity, and in bringing souls to Christ, even of those who have strayed far from the Christian faith.

TO CHRIST THROUGH MARY

It is commonplace in Catholic teaching to say that God wants us to come to His Son through Christ's Mother. What may be less obvious is that this has a unique application to priests.

This will seem less strange if we reflect on God's expectations of priests. He has entrusted them with the superhuman powers of transubstantiation in the Eucharist and of absolution in the sacrament of Penance. But because of these great privileges, He requires of them above ordinary holiness. Otherwise, as the Church's history sadly proves, the people will turn away from the sacraments which they see administered by unholy priests.

Yet holiness is impossible without grace, and priestly holiness without extraordinary grace. So that if by God's will, all the faithful somehow rely upon Mary to obtain the divine help which they need, priests more than others depend upon her to live up to the heavy demands made on them by Mary's Son. That is why priests can be frankly told that "God wants us to come to Him through Mary, so aspire by fervent prayer and self-discipline to take on her holiness even if it be with the help of the Blood of Christ. After all, her purity of soul and body is due to the prevision of the Blood of Christ. Our purity in chastity is due to the prevision of the Blood of Jesus Christ."[8]

As strange and as strong as the words may sound, it is no hyperbole for priests to say, "We must give ourselves to Mary so that we may belong entirely to God."

Experience shows how true this is. "If there is any unhappiness in the priesthood," as there is, "it is to be because of a lack of completeness of totality of giving." For "if I belong to God, I am bound for happiness because God is love, and if God is love I have the fullness of love." But how to give oneself thus entirely to God? The answer is "the Mother of God will help us to belong to God and to God alone." On one condition, that priests are devoted to this Mother and show their devotion by obeying her directive, first spoken to the servants at Cana, referring to her Son, "Do whatever He tells you." (John 2:5). If priests obey, miracles will happen in the sanctity of their own lives and in the graces that God will bestow on others through their apostolate. There is such a thing as offending the Blessed Virgin, not only by failing in due devotion to her, but mainly by not responding to the graces given to us by her Son, through the illuminations of His Spirit. "O Jesus," Father Gerald would pray, "we cannot bring pain to Thee without bringing sorrow to Our Lady. We cannot have need of a drop of Thy Precious Blood without having first matched Thy Blood with Thy Mother's bloodless agony."[9]

In practice, this means that "we must imitate and give up and give our souls to the Holy Ghost to love Our Lady with. How the Holy Ghost loves to fill the heart of a priest and the soul of a priest with love for the Mother of God, love for His stainless Spouse."[10] As a priest is more responsive to grace, he becomes more devoted to Mary; and as he grows in devotion to her, he becomes more generous in responding to the invitations of grace.

So great is Mary's love for souls that, like her Son, she has, if anything, a special predilection for those in sin — including priests estranged from God.

> Our Blessed Mother uses her heart as a pawn. She has given it over and over again, seeking even as Her Divine Son seeks with His Sacred Heart to win by love and tenderness the hearts of her sons beloved for Him. It is the tradition and the teaching of at least one of the mystics of the Church that Our Blessed Mother all through the public life showed a very special tenderness to Judas, thereby seeking to draw him away from the terrible disaster that was apparently to alienate his soul forever from his God. O final tenderness. O complete dedication to the purposes of the Redemption. The heart of the Mother of God showing special courtesy and tenderness, manifesting a predilection for the Apostle who was to betray her Son. How selfless is the heart of Mary that can so triumph over its natural feeling of resentment, and love even unto the last moment a soul that would betray its God.[11]

The lesson to be learned from this is that, like Mary, a priest should not show partiality in his affections. He is to show love "not only to the good but even to the malevolent, even to the wicked." "We must manifest towards them a great consideration. We must love them for what they could be even if we cannot love them for what they are, for the possibility of good that resides in them, for the possibility that we may some day salvage them for God."[12]

To illustrate this aspect of imitating Mary's compassion, Father Gerald recalled having just received a letter from a priest who at one time had to be dismissed from Via Coeli. And now, years later, after the grace of conversion touched his soul, he writes back with appreciation for the understanding care he was shown. "So," Father Gerald concludes, "consistently we must be good even to our enemies and thus follow closely in the footsteps both of Our Divine Master and of His beautiful Mother."[13]

PRACTICE OF PIETY

Internal devotion should find expression in practices of Marian piety in the life of a faithful priest — client of Our Lady.

Some of these practices are the common possession of all the faithful, others are more distinctively priestly. No matter, every one who is ordained by the Son of Mary is to manifest his special love for Christ's Mother.

Rosary. Paramount among these practices is the Rosary. Writers speak of the Rosary as the layman's breviary, and insofar as this indicates the devotion of our Catholic people to Our Lady, the designation is well justified.

> But is not the rosary a priest's Little Office? In the hands of his dear mother has it not channeled prayers for him from the time he was a heart-throb beneath her heart until he shall have joined her in the golden rosary of souls clustered at Mary's knee in Heaven? His own father said the beads for him before he was born. His own friends, including his priestly friends, have said and will say these same beads for him after he has passed into that purifying kingdom which we call Purgatory. Indeed if he himself lives long enough, dimming eyes will close to him the privileges of the chorusing of the inspired psalms but the rosary can still move through his fingers. In his mother's hands it guarded his cradle — in the hands of a Catholic Sister it will guard the cradle of his deathbed.[14]

No doubt, the Rosary belongs to the laity, but not exclusively. It is the property of all who belong to Mary, and who belongs to her by a higher right than her Son's priests?

> A priest is the follower of the Prince of Peace. The Rosary, a weapon of mercy, is his offensive weapon. With it,

like David with his sling with its five shining pebbles, he can overcome the Goliath of evil and liberate his own and the souls committed to his care. It is his walkie-talkie giving him instantaneous contact with the Queen of Heaven. It is a symbol of his priestly years slipping, bead by bead, through the Hands of God, slipping but never dropped, for God will not drop even the sinner while the sinner holds by the fingers of prayer the hem of Our Lady's robe of mercy. In short, if the Rosary is the layman's breviary it is as well a priests *vade mecum* — the symbol of his priestly consecration to a Queen and a Cause not of this world.[15]

Father Gerald was in the habit of reciting the fifteen decades of the Rosary every day, and he encouraged his followers to do the same.

Examen of Conscience. Not unlike the daily Rosary is the practice of the daily examination of conscience. This has been in the Church's heritage over the centuries. But what can make it distinctive for a priest is to make the review of his daily virtues and failings under the eyes of Mary.

Faith tells believers that the Blessed Virgin is aware of their conduct. Her eyes "rest upon us day by day, hour by hour, for it is a mother's privilege and duty to watch over her sons and daughters. And now from the high heaven, she watches over the world and in particular over the Christian world, and most particularly over those who on earth are by their vocation called upon to be other Christs."[16]

For a man who is willing to face the facts honestly, it would make a very searching and penetrating examen of conscience to ask himself: Have I brought joy or sorrow or have I even made it necessary for the Mother of God to turn her eyes from me this day? The examination of conscience is one of the standard practices of the spiritual life. It is one of the ways for the soul who is truly in earnest to make any progress, tries to check that progress. If we were runners we would carefully check our time for our daily trial run: so too the spiritual man who takes his life in earnest will check over his daily life, his record, his score sheet.

The eyes of Mary would make a very practical, very searching way of making that check. Our Blessed Mother saw my preparation for Mass — was she pleased with it? Our Blessed Mother saw and watched me during meditation — was she happy over it? Did she see my distractions? Our Blessed Mother saw my Mass — did it leave her happy? And so on through the day. O how supremely well a priest would have to live, to say honestly: I have held the smile in Our Lady's eyes, all day over my soul.[17]

Some may find these recommendations extravagant. But they were the normal expressions of a deep Marian faith that Pope John Paul II praised so highly on his pilgrim visit to the Shrine of Our Lady of Knock. Said the Holy Father, "I have been told that in Irish speech, the names of God and Jesus and Mary are linked with one another, and that God is seldom named in prayer or in blessing without Mary's name being mentioned also."[18] Father Fitzgerald had inherited this kind of faith.

<u>Days in Honor of Mary</u>. Another recommended form of devotion to the Blessed Virgin is to associate each day of the week with one of the Sorrows of Our Lady. "It goes very nicely especially when one puts Saturday as the repository, the taking down from the Cross, and Sunday as the entombment, giving Friday the place for the foot of the Cross, Thursday the meeting on the way to the Cross, Wednesday for the loss of the Christ Child, Tuesday for the fight into Egypt, and Monday for the first sorrow, Simeon's prophecy."[19]

On each day, the priest should give some special attention to the particular Sorrow of Our Lady and maybe compose a short prayer to go with it.

Thus on Mondays, as one finished for example the Hour of one's office, one would say, "The Sorrowful Heart pierced by the knowledge of Simeon's prophecy, grant that I may today console you by my fidelity to Christ."

Then on Tuesday, reflect on the flight into Egypt. "That flight into Egypt made our Blessed Mother Queen of all the D. P.s. What a Queen she is of all the displaced persons. So gather up all your little sorrows and separations from your dear ones. And you ought to say,

'Blessed Mother, I too am on my little flight into Egypt. Help me to travel lovingly and trustingly in Jesus and Joseph. And like Joseph, I trust in Jesus and in you.'"

On Wednesday, focus on "the loss of the Christ Child (that) ended in the finding of the Christ Child." The lesson is that "the joys and the sorrows in Our Lady's life are closely mingled, like our own lives." So that "if anybody goes with faith to our Divine Lord, the darkness is bound to disappear. We may not be with Him, but He is always with us."

Then on Thursday, "you have the meeting on the way to Calvary. Those of you who still have mothers on earth, you know that every moment that goes by brings one or the other of you closer to eternity." The mystery of Christ's meeting with Mary on the way to Calvary emphasizes the need for our own "great loving conformity to the Divine Will. We see everything pass: our life, our health, our opportunity. But please God before our opportunities pass, we must seize as many as we can for the salvation of immortal souls."

Friday is "the natural day to spend with Our Lady at the foot of the Cross." Among the sentiments to cultivate on Friday is the need for being patient with others, even as Mary was patient with her Son's executioners. "How blessed is the soul that learns to accept, to offer up the mortification of one's sensibility for the sake of Jesus. If we can't bring to God beautiful large gems of merit, let us bring the gold dust of our little sacrifices." In practice, this means we are to be "big in forgiving, big in overlooking the limitations of others, big in recognizing that behind every little man, stands the great beautiful God." To cultivate this habit, "Do what the Blessed Mother did: lifted her eyes over that crowd who were crucifying their God, over the heads even of the apostles, over the head of the golden hair of Magdalen, up to the Cross." She "lifted her eyes until they rested on Jesus." Then like Mary, you "will find in Jesus the answer to all your problems and permit Him as He did eventually for His Own Mother, to wipe away, to drive away, to absorb your tears in the golden chalice of His divine love."

Saturday commemorates the taking down from the Cross. "Who shall taste the sorrow of the Mother of God at the descent from the Cross? With a mother's privilege to be the throne of her child while in life, in death she became His altar."[20] This has particular meaning for priests who may see in the dead Christ in Mary's arms the numerous sinners estranged from God, and dead to His life, for whose reconciliation they have been mainly called to the priesthood.

Sunday may be associated with Christ's entombment, to commemorate Mary's strong faith while her Son's body was resting in the grave. It is also profitable spiritually to remember the poor souls in purgatory in relation to the seventh Sorrow of Mary. "Be devoted to the Queen of Purgatory, one of the titles of Our Lady."[21] Ask her to intercede for those who have died in body and are buried, but whose souls are still detained from heaven and especially "the priests to whose purgatory we may have contributed by our omissions or commissions."[22]

Sacrifice in honor of Mary. Anyone who understands the life of the Blessed Virgin realizes that the seven traditional Dolors by which she is honored did not exhaust the trials she underwent as the Mother of Sorrows. Just one example. Take the anguish "Our Lady must have felt, the fear and sorrow that must have gripped her heart when she went down to the synagogue at Nazareth with her Son whom everybody was talking about and He went up into the rostrum and opened the Book and began to speak." Then "before the day was ended, they tried to lynch Him; they tried to take His life."[23] All through Christ's life, from His birth in Bethlehem to His death in Jerusalem, Mary shared in His sorrows, and at every stage in the Savior's redemptive biography, His Mother suffered with Him and thus gave the faithful a pattern for imitation. That is why a good prayer to say is, "Dear Mother of Sorrows, pray for us that we may be worthy of a participation in the Passion of Christ."[24]

The more devoted a priest is to Mary the more his ingenuity will prompt him to offer some small sacrifice in her memory and to obtain, through her, the graces that he needs. Thus "abstaining in honor of Our Lady on Saturday is pleasing to Our Blessed Mother."[25] From the earliest Christian times, Saturday has been specially dedicated to the Blessed Virgin to commemorate her unswerving faith in her Son during the first Holy Saturday when He lay in the tomb. Others were disheartened because their faith in Christ failed them. But not Mary.

Besides external practices or simple progress, "Anything done, a triumph over self for Our Lady and ultimately for God", is commendable. Nothing we do is too trivial to "honor Our Lady, because God wills it." Moreover, "in honoring her we honor God," who is pleased with the veneration we pay His Mother.[26]

Can a priest ever be too devoted to Mary? Impossible. "How Jesus wants the hearts of His priests." Why should this be? Because "what Our Lord sees in the heart of a priest is the hearts of all the souls, the human beings, that He can reach through that priest." And how is a priest to give his heart to Jesus? 'We must imitate Mary."[27] She is the *Via immaculate* chosen by God to lead us to His Son. Consequently, "when you give your heart to Mary, you give it to Jesus most directly. When anyone gives himself or consecrates himself to the Immaculate Heart of Mary, our Blessed Mother straight — forwardly, immediately, without a moment's delay, deposits that heart in the Heart of her Son. She wants nothing for herself. The beautiful unselfishness we have seen in our own mothers is in its highest degree in the heart of Our Lady. She lives in heaven and she lives on earth only for the glory of God, only for the consolation of her Son's Heart, and so when she receives anything so precious as the heart of a priest, she immediately places that heart in the Heart of her Divine Son."[28]

Thus the classic phrase, *ad Jesum per Mariam,* to Jesus through Mary, is not only an expression of Catholic piety; it is the surest way of obtaining grace from Christ, for oneself and those for whose salvation we labor, by going to Him through His Mother. If there is one law in the spiritual life that should be memorized, it is that "we must give ourselves to Mary, so that we may belong entirely to God."[29] Devotion to her is the promise of surrender to her Son, who is the Son of God.

IX. THE HOLY HOUR

Father Gerald had a keen awareness, bordering on mystical experience, of Christ's abiding presence in the Holy Eucharist. When he drafted the Rule of Life for the Paracletes, he directed that they spend, "A personal Holy Hour daily, spent whenever this is possible in a chapel where Our Blessed Lord is present eucharistically. This is your Holy Hour given with Mary to Jesus."[1]

In his conferences to priests, whether his own Paracletes or others, he returned to the same directive: spend an hour a day before the Blessed Sacrament, besides the Mass and Divine Office. His praise of this practice, and the promises he assured those who followed it, were lavish, almost extreme:

A priest is to have an intense personal love of Our Lord. "Nowhere will that come to you, dear Fathers, so swiftly as in your quiet hours of adoration."[2]

A priest wants numerous graces from God. "Give God that hour and, if one places one's soul in the spirit of faith, of profound faith, in the presence of one's God, you will be surprised, pleasantly surprised, happily inundated by the graces your soul most needs."[3]

A priest is looking for support in his spiritual life. "If we ourselves can be faithful to a holy hour of prayer, especially a holy hour in the Eucharistic sunshine beneath the face of Christ in the golden Monstrance, and beneath His hidden sorrowful countenance, hidden beneath the veils of the tabernacle, we shall have a perpetual fervor. . . . If you are devoted to the Blessed Sacrament, you will never be long tried by dryness or the typical afflictions of spirit."[4]

A zealous priest must give up many natural pleasures and satisfactions. He therefore looks for supernatural compensation. "In your holy hour you will find the source of this joy. Here are the fountains of the Savior in which we must come to bathe our tired and parched souls and refresh our thirsting hearts."[5]

RECOMMENDED METHOD

If the holy hour is so important, it is well to know how to make it, at least to have some framework within which to pray before the Blessed Sacrament.

What Father Gerald recommends is only a suggestion. He recognizes that "as a soul advances in the spiritual life, all formal framework becomes less important." Still, it is useful for a priest to have some method available, for himself and for others whom he urges to undertake this basic Eucharistic devotion.

One method is based on the four word aspiration and prayer, *Adoro Te Rex Gloriae,* I adore Thee, King of Glory. The idea is to divide one's holy hour into four quarters: 'You spend the first in adoration; you spend the second in taking; you spend the third quarter in reparation; and finally you spend the last quarter in giving something to God."[6]

Adoration. Every prayerful posture of the soul before God should begin with adoration. In fact every prayer, no matter what other form it may take, is basically a form of adoration.

> The soul abases itself before the Divine Majesty and repeats quietly either verbally or in its own depths that offering: '*Adoro Te* — I like the repetition: *Adoro Te* — *adoro Te* — *adoro Te.* I adore You — I adore You — I adore You — with devotion. My God.' Now if a man has any depths of intellectual concept he does not need to get beyond that word God. My God! Thou who hast brought me out of nothingness.[7]

All around us, in the world of nature, are countless reasons for adoration. Or better, all around us the universe of space and time is adoring its Maker.

We see the majesty of the mountains round about us: we have our ear gradually attuned to the harmonies and symphonies that are going around — even down into the insect world. There is the whole voice of nature and it is a harmonious voice: little robins breaking their hearts with joy in the morning and saying thanks to God in the evening when they sing their vespers and compline. The majestic beauty of the moon as it moves — a symbol of the Mother of God, taking its light as Mary takes all from God, taking all its light from the sun — Mary takes her glory from the Son of God — and casting it into the dark; the beauty of the stars set as so many candles upon the altars of the universe.[8]

So it is. "All except God's rational creatures, do adore, according to their nature, even the stars singing in their orbits as they obey with exactitude the law of their Creator." Sublime thought, but also terrifying, that "All but men and angels, all but fallen men and fallen angels obey the rule of their Creator, the raison d'etre of their being."

This brings us back to the first purpose of the holy hour, to adore the Divine Majesty. Why should adoration before the Blessed Sacrament be specially commended and, for Father Gerald, be commanded to God's priests? The reason is not far to seek. It is hidden in the mystery of the Incarnation.

Father tells the priest that, by the power of his ordination, he brings down on earth today the same fullness of the Godhead corporally that came down to Palestine at the dawn of Christianity. This Godhead is therefore present near him, as near as was the Savior to His earthly contemporaries when they heard Him say, "I and the Father are one," or as was Thomas when he bowed down in adoration before the Risen Savior and acknowledged Him as "My Lord and my God."

We realize that this great infinite majesty of God has been gathered up and placed in the womb of a Virgin maiden and then by the beautiful, mystical extension of her virginity in fruitfulness the virgin priest of the Catholic Church and wombed in the golden tabernacle with the very same purpose that God the Creator without whom was made nothing that was made, from the bosom of His Father to the bosom of Mary and now to the bosom of the Church where we by our submission to the discipline of the Church have been privileged to bring forth in the fruitfulness that makes us even more than Joseph fruitful to God the Father in the bringing of His Son into the world: *Et Verbum caro Dictum est et habitavit in nobis* — and the Word was made flesh and dwelt among us.[9]

Recognizing who is present on the altar, the priest responds accordingly, and prays, "I adore Thee."

Petition. If adoration is the first attitude of a believing soul in the presence of the Word Incarnate, petition is the logical second. As a person realizes whom he is addressing, that it is the Lord of the Universe, here in human form; and he pauses to reflect on his own great misery, almost without reflection he will ask the Savior to give him what he needs.

Where to begin? Begin by asking Jesus, who is God, for His love.

What is the most precious thing that a man can have? To love Jesus. Without any doubt, without any qualification. To love God is God's greatest gift. As a matter of fact, the man who truly loves God with the proper motive, loves God for Himself, already possesses God and is already sure of heaven. For to love God is heaven — it is to possess heaven by anticipation. And not to love God is the commencement of hell. That is why there is so much unhappiness in the world.

So ask above all for the grace to love God and that will please Our Lord very much. It surprises Him for so many people to come to Him and ask Him so many things. Like the father in a family or a mother — the little ones come in during the day: Mother can I have a cookie — Mother, can I do this, Mother, can I do that? But suppose one little precocious child, very sweet and very thoughtful, didn't ask anything and the mother or dad said: All the others have asked for something, what do you want? And the little one said: Daddy, I just want to love you — I don't want anything except your love. Where is the father that would not catch up the little one and hold it tight to his heart? Where is the mother who would not be touched to the depth of her being by her little son or daughter who wanted nothing but to be loved?

This is the better gift, this is the gift that harmonizes with the philosophy and spiritual program of Saint Therese: she was avid and she was asking for the better grace, and the supreme grace is *caritas* — to love God. "In the bosom of the Church my Mother," she said, "I will be love." That is what she aspired to.[10]

Passing beyond the petition to love God, who is in the Eucharist as man out of love, priests are encouraged to pray for other priests, especially for those who are spiritually sick.

Father Gerald was always making references to the guest-priests at Via Coeli. He knew how desperately they needed the Eucharistic prayer of their brothers in the priesthood.

It just happens today that we had perhaps a record — the telephone rang more than five times — we have five priests about to come to Via Coeli — and what a sadness, for out of five priests, four of them are coming other than the first time. They are returning defeated, wounded, and we must set to work again. So we need the grace not to be discouraged; we need the grace to go on and on and on; we need the grace to whisper to our Lord: "Lord, you never were discouraged even though you knew that even up to the Last Supper, your chosen disciples whom you trained yourself would still be disputing who was going to be first in the Kingdom." They would be so slow to understand even in the Resurrection. Does not the dullness of the hearts of His Apostles call forth a cry from the Heart of Jesus? Does He not say: Slow of heart — ought not Christ to have suffered and so enter into His glory? Or as He upbraided them when He came through the barred doors in His glorified Body, on Easter Sunday, and He rebuked them for their tardiness to believe. So we must never be discouraged by human nature. And the only way not to be discouraged by human nature is to look with a very fixed look towards the Divine Master. Remember all the times that He has forgiven us — that He has pardoned us individually and out of the greatness of His patience with us, learn to be patient with these men of God who failed God over and over and over again.

Is it not true that only by great patience that Jesus has conquered in our individual lives? And if we then — if Christ has triumphed in our souls by patience, shall we find a better way to let Christ triumph for us in the souls of others? Then by patience upon patience upon patience — even when it is necessary for us to dismiss someone, let it not be because of our impatience, but because it has become evident that patience towards an individual must be sacrificed for the common advantage of the Community as a whole. Ask for priests who are dying obdurate and are refusing the sacraments, so that they may at the last moment capitulate to God's grace and be saved.[11]

But the prayer should be not only for priests. "Ask for your brothers and sisters in the world, ask for non-Catholics the grace of conversion, ask for dying sinners the grace that they make a little act of faith, perfect charity in their hearts." Then on a personal note, "Pray for the next one of your dear ones to die. Then when the telegram comes saying that someone has died suddenly, what a consolation. You don't know who, but you leave it in the hands of God."

Reparation. The next stage in the holy hour, which may actually pervade the whole sixty minutes, is the practice of reparation.

Preoccupied as he was with the moral failures of priests, Father Gerald specially urged priests (and all the faithful) to offer their prayers and trials for priests.

What reparation (is needed) for the sins of priests. O how precious to Christ is a priest who comes to Him and offers with his bare soul to wipe the terrible spittle and filth that unworthy priests cast each day upon Our Lord. It is true that the physical sufferings of Our Lord are at an end: but the source of those physical and mental anguishes that He bore in the Passion are today and tomorrow and all the tomorrows till the end of time. And it is effectively true that if I make reparation today, Jesus will see that reparation together with Veronica's reparation as He went the Way of the Cross. I went with the angel of consolation to Gethsemane — I went with Simon of Cyrene and lifted the cross from His aching shoulder — I was in the consolation that His Mother spoke to Him as He passed by — I was in the eyes of John when John lifted his lily face as a chalice to meet the eyes of Divine Love.

Learn the art of reparation and then the very little things that bother you, the little trivia of human limitations around us, the little contradictions and disappointments, can all be gathered up and offered in reparation — they become the myrrh of life.[12]

This art of reparation is mainly the practice of resignation. We resign ourselves to the trials and difficulties God sends us, and thereby expiate for the offenses committed against Him. Prayer before the Blessed Sacrament serves the purpose of motivating our wills and prayerfully uniting ourselves with Christ in the Eucharist, whose very presence on earth is a form of reparation.

Love. The final disposition of heart with which to keep the holy hour is affective charity.

In Father Gerald's vocabulary, gratitude and love are almost the same. We love God because He has so loved us. We thank Him for His goodness to us by our "goodness" to Him, that is by giving Him our hearts.

Speaking to priests bound to a life of celibacy, the exhortations to the love of Christ in the Holy Eucharist take on a special significance. "When you give your love to God you give Him that for which He created your heart: the reason He refused to give that heart up to the daughters of men." As a priest prays before the tabernacle, he is exercising his liberty in a way that no irrational creature can.

It is true the stars give their light and glory, but they cannot do otherwise. The birds sing their songs, but they cannot do otherwise; the flowers cannot help but be beautiful; the orchards cannot but be fruitful according to a fixed law. But you and I, dear Fathers, we can voluntarily, willingly give something to God. And what can a man give to God that He does not already possess? We can give Him our love.[13]

This is consistent with the Church's traditional understanding of the four ends of the Mass: adoration, petition, reparation and grateful love. Worship of the Holy Eucharist reserved on the altar should take on the same four ends. As a priest gets into the habit of making his daily holy hour, his daily Mass will take on a deeper meaning. It will also gain for him other priests, and the faithful the graces that the Redeemer intends to confer through the sacrifice-sacrament of the Mass.

X. Priestly Celibacy

The combined published and recorded words of Father Gerald amount to several hundred thousand words, perhaps a million or more. And yet one of the remarkable features of all this public discourse, there is relatively little on the subject of priestly chastity or celibacy.

It cannot be that he was not painfully conscious of the problem that celibacy poses in the life of a priest. His years of experience with "priests in trouble" were enough to convince him, as he admitted, that fidelity to his celibate commitment makes a heavy, sometimes heroic, demand on the generosity of one who wants to remain faithful to the Christ who ordained him. One reason for the relative silence on this subject was perhaps the realization that we are here dealing with a very delicate matter, so delicate, in fact, that it should not be lightly treated in public. Moreover, as those who knew Father Gerald best can testify, he did often deal with chastity among priests, but in a manner that would be most beneficial to the persons in question, namely in private and with the protection of confidentiality.

There was some value in making these preliminary observations. At least they will serve the purpose of emphasizing the profound wisdom of Father Gerald's insights on an issue that, thanks to the media, is one of the most agitated in the Catholic Church today.

CHURCH'S TEACHING

Father Gerald began with the premise that marriage and conjugal love are beautiful and pleasing to God. If Christ invites some people to follow Him in consecrated chastity, "it is not that there is anything unholy about married life; on the contrary, it is a very, very holy state. The fact that people abuse it does not change God's plan; parents, husband and wife, should themselves be angels, and there is

105

nothing unholy, in the least way unholy, in the way God has chosen by human love incorporated with divine love to bring beautiful souls into this world."[1]

This deserves to be stressed, because part of the propaganda against celibacy is the charge that, somehow, the Church is Manichaean in her attitude toward sex. She forbids priests in the Roman Rite to marry, so the critics claim, because marriage in her eyes is unclean.

But the Church's stand on celibacy is not based on a lie. It is founded on a truth, revealed truth; which also explains why the Church is so adamant. "We live in a world that challenges on every level the ideal and the virtue, the angelic virtue of chastity." It is not surprising, then, that "there is pressure on Rome at all times for the lifting of the discipline of chastity, absolute chastity. Rome has been petitioned in our own lifetime from several different parts of the world for the elimination of the discipline of priestly celibacy. And yet the Church will not take this step," in spite of the pressure and notwithstanding the failure of not a few priests to live up to their celibate commitment.[2]

The basis for the Church's teaching on priestly celibacy is the unique example of Christ, the great High Priest, and His teaching about the sacrifice of marriage "for the sake of the Kingdom of Heaven" (Matthew 19:12).

SOURCE OF PRIESTLY CHASTITY

If the example and teaching of the Savior during His visible stay on earth are the historic ground for the Church's discipline on celibacy, the grace that comes from Christ in the Holy Eucharist sustains the priest in his faithfulness to a lifetime of celibacy.

Jesus in the Blessed Sacrament is the very source of our purity, the source of our strength, which makes it possible for a human soul to lift itself. We are offered in exchange for the renunciation of human love and human consolation, we are offered not angelic love, we are offered Divine Love. We are offered the ultimate love of the human entity. Any human rational relation that is to attain to happiness, is going to attain to happiness in God, in God and in God alone.[3]

Faith tells the priest that in the Blessed Sacrament is really, truly and substantially present the living Son of God in human form.

> As a matter of fact, here is heaven, a veiled heaven, here is the actuality of a Divine Lover. Now our hearts are built to love, and one of the fruitful causes of defection in the priesthood, is the failure to fill up the vacuum that is created by the vow of chastity with another love. A man is bound to love something, he may deny it, but ordinarily that type of man who denies the necessity of love in his life, will seek the most terrible and ugly of all loves which is the love of his own ego, the love of self. A man who loves something and where we have pledged ourselves not to give our hearts to creatures at least in that most intimate and strong love that the chords of Adam draws towards, the marriage union, we must sublimate our hearts into a love and a love that is offered us, a legitimate love for the priest's heart is the Blessed Sacrament, Our Lord.[4]

It is impossible to exaggerate the importance of elevating one's affections above earthly desires and center them on Christ, present in the Eucharist, as a condition for celibate fidelity. "If a priest loves the Blessed Sacrament enough, he will sacrifice," besides other virtues, "the attractiveness of human love."

At this point, Father Gerald told an anecdote that forcefully brings out the lesson he wants to teach others. "When I was a young priest," he recalled, "I made it a practice in parish life, whenever I married a couple — I married many attractive young couples — I always would slip around afterwards to the back of the tabernacle and kiss the tabernacle and thank God that He had not given my heart to a creature but to Himself."[5] If this self-disclosure tells us something about the person who revealed it, it tells us more about the truth he was trying to convey.

Implicit in this insistence on cultivating a deep personal love for Christ is a deep-seated tendency in human nature that needs to be supernaturalized.

Man was made to adore and in human love there is a tendency to exaggerate into adoration, love of creature for creature. Now here is where we have an advantage over those in other walks of life. Our brothers and sisters who are married in the world they must love with a very supreme love their life-partners and they must be careful, if their partner is a fine Christian product, they have to be careful not to adore. We don't have to take that precaution, in loving Christ we can adore, we must adore, we should adore, He is the perfection of the God-head revealed to men in human form. Here is a perfect lover, here is a perfect companion, here is a perfect comrade for love. And you cannot love Him too much, you cannot adore Him too much, you cannot serve Him too perfectly, you cannot rely upon Him too much, He will never fail you. You can fail Him, I can fail Him, we can fail Him, but He will never fail us.[6]

There is more implied here than a bit of psychology. It is not only that by raising his mind and heart to God, a priest sublimates his natural appetites and thus masters his bodily passions.

Locked up in this recommendation in capsule form is the Church's two millennia of teaching. St. Augustine's prayer, "Thou hast made us for thyself, O Lord, and our hearts are restless until they rest in Thee," is literally true. And it can be proved to be true from experience, even in this life: that a person whose faith is strong enough will find fulfillment in the love of God beyond any satisfaction that the love of creatures can provide.

Along with a strong attachment to the person of Christ and ardent devotion to the Real Presence, a life of celibacy needs the daily nourishment that comes from receiving the Body and Blood of the Savior.

We have undertaken to sacrifice the comforts of home life, we, like Joseph, found ourselves in the situation that demands of us absolute integrity, absolute holiness of life. There is no use to circumvent the truth, we are called upon to live the life of angels. And that is why the Son of God has given us the bread of angels, that is why He pours in every Holy Communion we receive, He pours into our poor, animal, lusting bodies His Divine angelic virginity. He gives us a blood transfusion, not of a pint, but of the fullness of His own Body and His own Blood, in order to strengthen us, in order to incorporate us into His own holiness. And in our battle to maintain this heroic virtue, this virtue that calls in most instances for men, for heroic living, this virtue that makes, by reason of the faith of our people in us, us honored above all other men, we must make use of this help of God, we must make use of this Divine auxilium.[7]

As by now centuries of priestly experience has shown, to remain constant in consecrated chastity requires superhuman power of detachment from creatures and attachment to God. Only supernatural means, such as the Sacrament of the Eucharist provides, are adequate to meet this superhuman need.

THE INSPIRATION OF MARY AND JOSEPH

If the primary source of grace to maintain oneself chaste is the Holy Eucharist, as Presence, Communion and Sacrifice, the corresponding source of inspiration is devotion to the Blessed Virgin Mary and St. Joseph.

In one sentence, priests are told that, "Here is a simplification for holy living, for virginal living, for chaste living, to live under the gaze of our Blessed Mother."

This living under the gaze of Mary is no poetic effusion. It is stark reality, as by now thousands of priests have faithfully done and immensely benefited themselves and the Church from the practice. Underlying the special devotion to Mary that should characterize priests more than anyone else in the Church is the comparison, based on faith, between Mary's role in the Incarnation and the priest's role in making possible the Holy Eucharist.

It was, indeed, ineffable that God should have chosen to be conceived and born of the Virgin Mary, "That God should do this for one chosen individual, that He should come using divine power and the Blood of the Lamb, that He should do this for a single soul is hardly conceivable." But what happened at Nazareth and Bethlehem was only a foreshadowing of more marvels still to come. The divine plan was still more universal.

> God is infinite and He not only would take a single crea-
> ture and grant her the privilege of giving of her flesh and
> blood that the Son of God might live on earth, walk on
> earth clothed in our humanity, like unto us in all save sin,
> but here is the miracle, the mystery miracle in the Catho-
> lic Church: the extension of the mystery of the divine In-
> carnation, not through the stainless Mother of God, but
> now in time through you and through me, dear Fathers.

> God willed to deal through time, if I might say so with
> reverence, not with the will of the Immaculate, but with
> your will and my will.

> A priest, sinful man, would thus pave the way for Christ,
> the Son of God, the stainless Man of God, to live and
> work and absolve and pray to His Father and intercede for
> man unto the end of time. Therefore, what Mary did once
> in the Incarnation, we have the privilege of doing all
> through the centuries, through the waves of the ocean of
> time.[8]

Of course, Mary was the all-holy Mother of God, whereas priests are, with emphasis, sin-laden servants of the Lord. But she recognizes, better than anyone under God, the dignity of her Son's priests, and the importance of their chastity — to be modeled on hers. She wants them to be fruitful in spiritual offspring, comparable to her own supernatural fecundity. After the example of Mary, "so the priest, day by day brings forth Jesus. He is fruitful in virginity and he is fruitful in proportion to his virginity. Where is the Church most loved? Where are her priests most distinguished in the holiness of their living?" Where they are most Marian in their practice of chastity. "Par excellence, by choice, by predilection the Son of God wishes to be born of virgin bodies and virgin souls."[9]

After the Mother of God, a priest's highest inspiration should be Mary's chaste spouse, St. Joseph. What endears the Foster-Father of Jesus to priests is the sublime example he gave of living a virginal life and thus cooperating in a unique way in the foundations of Christianity.

There are numerous points of contact and similarity between the life of a priest and the life of Joseph as the chaste Guardian of the Virgin and the putative father of the Son of God. And all the similarities rest on the basic fact that Joseph lived a life of consecrated chastity.

> The Priest of God, like Joseph, is called to a special manner of life, to a virgin love and a virgin life in the company and companionship of Jesus and Mary. Joseph stands before him as a shining example of that tender yet strong and energetic character that should be the goal of his priestly training. Joseph held Jesus day by day in his strong pure hands: so too, does the Priest. Joseph guarded the stainless honor of God's Own Spouse, the Blessed Virgin; a priest in active service guards first the honor of his own soul espoused to God, and then as well the souls, the sweet, innocent souls of many, many of the virgin spouses of God's Spirit.[10]

St. Joseph proves what every priest needs to believe, that what is impossible to nature is possible with grace; that first as Mary was both Virgin and Mother, so Joseph was both Virgin and Spouse. Consecrated chastity is beyond the powers of nature; it is the achievement of God. But what God worked in the Spouse of Mary, He can also accomplish in those dedicated to her Son, provided, like Mary, they believe that nothing is impossible with God.

SAFEGUARDS OF CHASTITY

Consistent with his emphasis on the human will and the importance he attached to freedom, Father Gerald told priests that chastity must be worked at to be achieved. You do not preserve your celibacy merely by prayer or sublime motivation. "Guard your chastity," he said. "You live in a world which is growing daily more and more pagan, and worse than pagan in its positive immodesty."

What is modesty? "Modesty is a distinctively Christian virtue, although you will find the instinct of it in nature. But modesty comes from a recognition of original sin. It does not deny the beauty of a creature; we proclaim it. Man is in the image of God, man and woman. No wonder nature is attractive; it is the image of God. But we must learn, in the midst of the beauty and attractiveness of the world, to lift the eyes of our soul and fasten and feed them upon an eternal and most consoling truth," the beauty of the uncreated God, who made His creatures so beautiful.

The first safeguard of chastity, therefore, is the practice of Christian modesty by moderating the internal and external movements according to one's station in life, here as a priest. Above all a priest must keep modesty of the eyes, which are the window of the soul. He must realize that, having a fallen human nature, he cannot read, or watch, or look at anything or anyone that appeals to him, without danger to his celibate consecration.

Along with modesty goes reverence for one's own and other people's bodies. "We must learn to respect the temples of the Holy Ghost."[11] Reverence will incline us to show honor and respect for persons because of the dignity they all possess. Their bodies, even when naturally unattractive are shrines of the Holy Trinity; and no matter how attractive, are as nothing compared to the ravishing beauty of the God who made them. In either case, priests must "remember that we are dedicated not to the shadow of Divine Beauty, which is in man, but to the reality of Divine Beauty which is in Jesus Christ." To keep ourselves chaste, "we must live by faith, and by faith sublimate our souls to the Divine Beauty that death will reveal to us."[12]

Finally and summarily, to maintain one's celibacy, a priest has to develop a strong spiritual life. This is more than the casual statement of the fact might indicate.

As Father Gerald viewed the service of God, the spirit of man under the influence of grace was not only on the highest level among human possessions, but it dominated man's lower powers. What occasioned the long passages that follow was a report in the public press, quoting some Catholic authority to the effect that it is not enough to provide for a man's spiritual and physical life. He also had an emotional life to be cared for. With this, Father Gerald strongly disagreed.

If a man's spiritual life is what it ought to be, it **dominates** his emotional life. A man's spiritual life that does not dominate his emotional life is worth nothing. God gave us an immortal soul in the primacy of the spirit. And if a man's soul belongs to God, then his emotional life will be subordinated, and he will dominate his passions as did St. Paul and all the other saints of God! St. Augustine knew the sweetness of the arms of a woman, but he broke that embracement. By what? By his spiritual life! By the correspondence of his soul to grace![13]

By the spiritual life is meant living in such a way that "God becomes uppermost in a soul." Then, a person "has that with which to dominate." Then grace is at work to master fallen nature. But "if he cannot dominate his emotional life, if he cannot dominate his lust for women," then it must be said "he has not a dominant spiritual life. He does not belong body and soul to Christ. And the only security for a man, in the priesthood or in the laity, for a man to save his soul, is that Christ the Son of God be dominant in his life."[14]

If we want to know what power the spirit, under grace, has over nature, look at St. Paul, who said, "I live, no not I, but Christ liveth in me." (Galatians 2:20). St. Paul knew what he was talking about. He knew our emotional life: "I find the law of my members striving against the law of my mind, and trying to captivate me in sin. But I am what I am by the grace of God." (Romans 7:22-23, I Corinthians 15:10).

The lesson for the preservation of chastity is plain. As a man labors to make Christ dominant in his life, God will give him the strength, especially through the Eucharist, to dominate his passions.

When a man has a valid and authentic spiritual life, if that dominates his soul, then he will be saved by the grace of God. You cannot separate in a living human entity soul and body and mind and heart. One is going to dominate, and it is our philosophy that a man will find security by bringing his soul and anchoring it here at the feet of Jesus, who is in the world for that very purpose: that men may find here, in the Shadow of the Rock, the peace and the calm and the shade and the rest. And like Moses, they may strike that Rock and out will gush the Precious Blood in the daily Mass for the inebriation for our souls with a higher inebriation than any creature or created entity can give us.[15]

This is not to say there will not be a struggle, or that nature is easily tamed. It does mean, however, that we look in the right place for the power to tame our rebellious nature and that we use the appropriate means. The power needed to remain faithful to the chaste Christ must ultimately come from Christ, as He Himself foretold. "Not everyone," He declared, "can accept what I have said, but only those to whom it is granted" (Matthew 19:11). And among the means by which "it is granted," none are more effective than the graces given by the Savior, when He gives Himself to us in the Blessed Sacrament of the altar.

XI. PRAYING FOR PRIESTS

Father Gerald was too familiar with the Scriptures not to know how important is prayer in the apostolate to priests. What he read in the New Testament convinced him that priests must personally be men of prayer, but others must — imperatively must — pray for them.

St. Luke tells the story of King Herod's persecution of the early Church; how after he beheaded James the brother of John and saw that this pleased the Jews he decided to arrest Peter as well. "He put Peter in prison, assigning four squads of four soldiers each to guard him in turn. Herod meant to try Peter in public after the end of Passover week. All the time Peter was under guard the Church of God prayed for him unremittingly" (Acts 12:2-5).

In like manner, St. Paul, in what is considered his first inspired letter, closed the epistle to the Thessalonians with the earnest plea, "Pray for us, my brothers" (I Thessalonians 5:25).

Here we have the revealed teaching of the Holy Spirit, as a practice (for Peter) and a petition (by Paul) that among the duties of a Christian is to pray for priests. Surely if Peter, the first Pope, and Paul, the Apostle to the Gentiles, needed prayers, how much more their successors in the papacy, episcopate and the priesthood.

And most recently, when Pope John Paul II was elevated to the papacy, the day after his election he preached at the Mass he concelebrated with the College of Cardinals. The highpoint of his homily was an urgent request for prayers. "After praying to the Lord," he said, "we feel the need of your prayers to gain that indispensable heavenly strength that will make it possible for us to take up the work of our predecessors from the point where they left off."[1]

All of this and more is part of the Church's unbroken tradition, since the earliest Christian times. The faithful pray for their priests, from the Bishop of Rome to the least known curate in some mapless village on the other side of the world. They are all "the anointed of the Lord."

We have already seen how plainly the founder of the Paracletes and Handmaids saw this need. In fact we might say this was the main reason he established the two religious institutes; that their members might pray for priests and they, in turn, might inspire other thousands of the faithful everywhere to do the same. On a personal note, this was also the main reason why the present author wrote this book on Father Gerald: to motivate people to pray, as they have never done before, for priests. In my estimation here is the principal neglect in Catholic Christianity today: even as praying to God for priests *unremittingly,* offers the greatest hope for the Catholic Church of tomorrow.

WHY PRAYER

As we begin to ask ourselves, "Why should the faithful pray for priests?", the first response is also the fundamental one. Since all the faithful, priests included, are members of the same Mystical Body, all should cooperate with one another for the upbuilding of this Body and the greater glory of God.

Each of us has a different task to perform in the Church of Christ, and each has his or her own responsibility, according to their state of life. We should pray that fathers and mothers be good parents; wives and husbands good spouses; that children be good children; that the unmarried and widows serve God in their respective positions; that religious be good religious and faithful to their vocation.

So, too, priests deserve to be prayed for, just because they are priests and therefore part of the visible society, which is the Church. She is made up of many, and different members, each needing the other and each depending on the others for prayerful support.

But priests have been chosen to serve a unique and especially exalted role in the Mystical Body. They are to perpetuate the sacrifice of Calvary in the Mass, make present the living Christ on earth in our day and, in the power given them by Christ, they are to absolve the contrite of their sins. Yet all the while they remain human, very human beings, and therefore in need of divine assistance in the form of actual grace. To obtain this grace and sustain them even in God's friendship, they themselves must pray, and no one can substitute for this primary law of our faith. Either priests pray, or, like anyone else, they will fall into temptation. Yet that is not enough. They also need the supporting prayers of others, and they have a special claim on this support because of what their ministrations mean to the people.

The faithful are rightly enamored of the Church's great treasures and of the blessings that she brings to her children. But who mainly dispenses these gifts of God to His people?

> In all this glory and all this throbbing vitality that leads souls to eternal life — in this beautiful door, we have the mystical Christ. But who gives us the mystical Christ? It was the priest who baptized me and through this door I will pass into eternity. So the priest plays such a vital part, we might say, if a priest understands and is true to his vocation, he is Christ in the world today.[2]

Gratitude, therefore, should prompt us to pray for those who have been such benefactors in our lives. Father Gerald was addressing the Handmaids but, through them, he was speaking to everyone.

> Therefore — and keep this as a memory when we are far apart — since Christ, who is Eternal Wisdom and Eternal Love, has deliberately chosen to use men for such a vital role, anytime anyone strengthens that priest or all priests, strengthens the very Hand of Christ — the Heart of Christ — the Lips of Christ — the Eyes of Christ. Now this is the reason and it should be the inspiration of your particular vocation. If a priest goes promptly on a sick call tonight, see the value of your vocation. If your prayer is universal, he is a priest strengthened by your prayers — the graces that have come from your prayers to him. You have helped Christ on that sick call if you are praying for priests and praying according to their needs in the Heart of Christ, you have helped today, the poor shivering ill-

clad priest in Siberia, you have helped the faithful hiding
in their hideouts in China.[3]

Then an astounding statement, but based on the faith. "All the
vocations, everything stems through the priesthood of Christ." But
this priesthood is not only a memorable fact of past history. Certainly Christ died and merited our salvation on Good Friday. Yet His
priesthood continues today. He is even now communicating the graces
He won for us on the Cross. And the principal channel of this communication is the Sacrifice of the Mass in which He uses human
beings, His priests, to distribute the blessings of Calvary. "Christ
Himself at the altar comes to Mass by the hands of a priest." What
follows? Consequently, "in strengthening the priest you strengthen
the whole Church." In other words, "strengthen the priest and you
strengthen the whole foundation," from one viewpoint, or "the whole
roof," from another viewpoint. In a word, "you strengthen everything in the Church."[4]

Years before he founded any religious community, Father Gerald
was already telling people the same thing. "Hour by hour," he said,
"somewhere the Mass is always being offered. And wherever the
Mass is being offered, because of the One who is offering it, God
through the Mass is attaining at every moment a greater glory than
all the rest of us adopted children could take away from Him." This
offers a second powerful motive why the faithful should pray for
priests, to insure that God be continuously, and in the highest degree,
glorified by the re-enactment of Calvary.

How will prayer contribute to this divine praise? By warding
off the evil spirit who sees in the Mass the greatest hindrance to his
demonic activity. "Therefore, it is the Mass that counts, and that is
why the arch-enemy of God tried to destroy it as far as he could at the
time of the Reformation, and still tries to eliminate the Mass and the
priesthood, the priesthood and the Mass."[5]

The devil knows that every Mass gives immeasurable glory to
the Divine Majesty, which he hates. So he does everything in his
power to seduce priests into his camp so they will not offer Mass, or
offer it less often, or less devoutly; anything to prevent God being
given the glory and souls from receiving the graces that flow from
the Holy Sacrifice of the Mass.

That is why believing Catholics are not surprised to be told, "you must always in your secret espousal of God's cause, in work ing for God's cause, always carry a special place in your prayers and in your heart for the sanctification of the priesthood and the sacred- ness of the Mass."[6] The two go together. Every prayer for the sancti- fication of priests, to protect them from the malice of the devil, is a prayer for the greater glory of God through the Mass which priests alone can offer to the Heavenly Father.

A moment's reflection should tell a believer that "the priest- hood is a terrifying exaltation." That is why, "you can do nothing more consoling to His Sacred Heart than to pray for His priesthood; for by the institution of the priesthood God has committed His stain- less honor, His deepest interests, to the keeping of created clay." Among the saints, "St. Teresa of Jesus knew this and that is why she made prayers for the priesthood the first duty of her Carmelite fam- ily. A faithful priest is God's greatest consolation, an unfaithful priest the source of His deepest sorrow."[7] Then speaking for himself, Fa- ther Gerald asked, "I would beg one decade of the Rosary each day, thanking Mary for my vocation and asking that I may be each day nearer and dearer to her Heart and to her Son Divine."[8]

PRIESTS IN SIN

If prayer is so important for priests in general, it is urgently needed for those who have strayed from their high calling. True to his own injunction, not to discuss the sins of priests without real necessity, Father Gerald said very little publicly about the failings of those whom he was so zealous to bring back to the path of virtue. Yet when it came to moving his own followers or others to pray for priests, he did not hesitate to point out, in stark terms, how absolutely indis- pensable was prayer, much prayer if the shepherds of the flock were to be restored to their priestly life and dignity.

Statements abound in which Father Gerald makes no secret of the malice of sin in a priest, and of the harm he does to the Church by his infidelity. "Who has struck the beautiful spouse of Christ? What has disfigured the spouse of Christ? The sins of priests."[9]

Unworthy priests are more than a source of scandal to the faith- ful. They renew the mockery of the Mystical Christ today, even as the Roman soldiers mocked the physical Christ during His Passion on Holy Thursday night.

> Those poor soldiers, all they thought was that Jesus was a poor dreamer, a poor seer and perhaps, a half-wit, a poor victim of the mob who was given to them that they might have some fun according to their ideas of fun. As cruel men sometimes cast a poor little rabbit to the hounds after they have caught it, or a poor little mouse to the cat to be played with, they did not know that this was the King of Kings.

> But, when I or another priest of God do anything unworthy, I step up to Him and bow my knee in mockery, and make the world laugh. The world who hates Christ and does not believe. They smile and say, "There is your priest for you." I set the crown back hard and deep into the Sacred Seat of Divine Wisdom. Oh, this is a mystery of suffering that is especially continued through time.

> How Christ suffers in being mocked in the person of His priest! It is too late for a priest to make a decision, would to God it was not, it is too late for a priest to turn back and be something else.[10]

But they cannot be anything else. They are ordained for ever. And even if they try to forget, the world never forgets. It knows, as by supernatural instinct, what a priest should be and if he shows himself unfaithful, the whole Church suffers by the counter witness he gives to everyone who enters his life.

It follows, then, that the sins of priests are particularly offensive to God.

> There is a passage in the Psalms that applies especially to sin in a priest. The Psalmist says, "I was wounded in the house of a friend." If ever there is a place that should be the house of a friend, it should be the soul of a priest. It should be a house that is given over as a true friend gives over his home when a friend comes to him; so before all else a priest's soul belongs to Christ. It should be the house

of his friend. And there the wounds that He receives by the sins of a priest all represent a special depth of anguish; they have a special poignancy to Our Lord because He loves so much.[11]

Not everyone is aware of the sins of priests. And it is just as well. Those who are aware may in one sense be said to be privileged; but what is more important, they assume a grave responsibility.

If we become aware of the infidelities of priests, the ingratitudes of priests, the coldness and sinfulness of priests, we have the privilege of being invited, as it were, into the very depths, the deepest sorrows of the Sacred Heart, the sorrows that He will not reveal to the world.

Think of all the millions of devout Catholics who are not even aware — as I practically up to my ordination — was unaware that there was any such thing in the world today, as a priest who was unfaithful to his obligations. So wholesome, so healthy, so faith-filled was the little parish where I was brought up and the parishes in which I was brought up that I was not aware that a priest today could wound the Sacred Heart as I now know the Sacred Heart is wounded.[12]

No doubt the press and media have in recent years publicized the sins of priests on a scale that was not known, or even knowable, before. Nevertheless, no matter how notorious grave public sin may be in a priest, it is still such a "terrible scandal." Why? Because people look to their priests to be holy; indeed they have a right to expect as much.

Given the fact that the deepest sorrows of Christ's Heart are the scandals that involve His "other selves," His priests whom He has so loved and has so desired to draw into the highest sanctity, "How then shall we respond?" It should be the response "that a son or daughter would make; would go over and take the mother's hand and say, 'Never mind, mother, I'll make up for the one that has hurt you. I'll make reparation. I'll pay that bill. I'll take up that burden. I'll lighten your cross.'" In a word, the evidence of infidelity in priests should arouse in the hearts of Christ's faithful the wish to expiate.

At the core of Father Gerald's apostolate to priests was this desire to repair for their sins. And those who were to follow him as Paracletes or Handmaids, he urged to be "dedicated to reparation." They were told "little by little, learn to disdain the ordinary satisfactions of life." Why reparation? Because "this devil in the priestly heart is cast out only by prayer and fasting."[13] Not by prayer alone, but by prayer and mortification. This need not mean extraordinary bodily austerities. But it does mean the patient endurance of whatever trials the Lord may send; or the withdrawal of the pleasures and satisfactions previously had; or the silent endurance of rejection and mistrust; or the quiet bearing up with a painful illness, disability or wasting disease. What form the mortification takes is secondary. What is primary is the will to expiate. And this will should become imperative: "Progressively and always with the restraint that is guided by humble obedience to spiritual direction and to superiors, way down deep we must develop a thirst for reparation; and it will come logically in the supernatural order, as we grow in the love of Jesus Christ."[14]

All of this makes sense only on the premises of faith. The more deeply a person believes that all sin demands expiation, and the sins of priests are especially odious to God, the more readily will he want to repair the damage done to the Church and to souls by voluntary reparation. All the while the believer knows that, not only is the divine honor vindicated but the sinner himself, here the priest, is showered with graces of divine mercy to become reconciled with God.

If this privilege of reparation is pleasing to God from everyone, it is particularly welcome when the one who expiates is himself a priest, making up for his fellow priests who are estranged from God. Father Gerald recommended identifying this kind of priest-for-priest reparation with the Sixth Station of the Cross, and associating it with one's daily Holy Hour before the Blessed Sacrament.

> Then you come to the great beautiful field of reparation. What a privilege! A beautiful symbol of Veronica pushing her way through the lineup as it were, making a special effort, going to Our Lord and lifting her veil and receiving in return the beautiful image of Christ. Lift your soul. O what reparation for the sins of priests. O how precious

to Christ is a priest who comes to Him and offers with his bare soul to wipe the terrible spittle and filth that unworthy priests cast each day upon Our Lord. It is true that the physical sufferings of Our Lord are at an end, but the source of those physical and mental anguishes that He bore in the Passion are today and tomorrow and all the tomorrows till the end of time. And it is effectively true that if I make reparation today, Jesus will see that reparation together with Veronica's reparation as He went the Way of the Cross.

Learn the art of reparation and then the very little things that bother you, the little trivia of human limitations around us, the little contradictions and disappointments, can all be gathered up and offered in reparation. They become the myrrh of life.[15]

This, in fact, is the essence of devotion to the Precious Blood. It means that we unite our shedding of blood, in spirit if not in body, with the bloody Passion of Christ, and thus effectively draw God's mercy on the sinners, including priests, for whom we expiate.

XII. Caring for Priests

There are two sides to Father Gerald's apostolate to priests. One side is universal and reaches out to all bishops and priests in the Church, in fact not only the living but also the deceased. Its object is to solicit the divine mercy and obtain for priests the grace they need, among the living to become holy, and for the deceased a speedy release from purgatory. On this level, all the faithful are asked to cooperate. By their prayers and sacrifices they merit before God what the Lord promises to give those who ask in His name. And if anything can be asked for in the name of Christ, it is certainly the blessings of His goodness on those whom, from eternity, He has chosen to anoint with the powers of the priesthood.

The other side of the apostolate is more specific and restricted. Its scope is to help priests who have wandered from the path of virtue, whether of faith, hope or charity, and strive to bring them back, at least to God's friendship and, if possible, to the exercise of their priestly ministry.

Another name for this second side of the apostolate is "Caring for Priests." Its presence in the Church as an organized effort is relatively new, and in the United States may be said to have started with Father Gerald Fitzgerald when he established the Servants of the Paraclete.

Enough has been said so far to give some explanation of why such an apostolate should have waited until the mid-twentieth century. Of course some priests who had strayed from their calling had been the object of the Church's concern over the centuries; and there was never a time when she was not solicitous to help those who had difficulties living up to their priestly responsibilities. But the inroads of secularism in the Church's ranks, including the priesthood, had not been so widespread or at least there were not as many priests affected in former days as all the evidence points to being true today. Two world wars, with some thousands of priests, either conscripted or as chaplains, contributed to the weakening of priestly morale. Moreover, as was mentioned before, the affluence of certain cultures, as in Western Europe and America, further undermined the strength of the priestly vocation.

Whatever the reasons, and they are both numerous and complex, the net result has been too obvious to deny or even ignore. There have been many casualties, as we say, among priests; in some cases as many as half the ordination class in a large diocese. Clearly priests need to be helped, and helped urgently, if the work of the Church in countries like ours is to even survive let alone prosper and grow in serving the People of God.

It is to Father Gerald's credit that he had the vision and the courage to undertake what he did. It is impossible to overemphasize the magnitude of his pioneer efforts to rehabilitate priests, or the prophetic vision he must have had to foresee the needs of the Church into the twenty-first century. He died in 1969, less than four years after the close of the Second Vatican Council, and therefore when the full impact of the post-conciliar revolution had not yet been felt.

In order to better understand and appreciate his apostolate of caring for priests it seems wise to see it first from the perspective of the late Pope John XXIII, who personally evaluated Father Gerald's approach and methodology, and warmly praised it; and then in the words of Father Gerald himself, drawing on his numerous directives to those whom he associated with himself and inspired to vow themselves to serve Christ in His priests.

POPE JOHN XXIII

It is surely a credit to the founder of Via Coeli that less than ten years after the Paracletes were formally approved as a religious congregation, Pope John XXIII issued a detailed personal letter "To Our Beloved Son, Gerald of the Holy Spirit," praising not so much him personally as the work he was doing for priests and the way he was doing it. "Our pastoral heart was greatly consoled," the Pope began, "when we learned of your commendable apostolate among the Lord's anointed who, while bearing 'the heat of the day and the burden' (Matthew 20:12), have fallen a prey to the insidious snares of evil that beset the paths of priests." Immediately, therefore, the Pope set the tone to his letter of commendation by focusing on the one phase of this apostolate that Father Gerald spent twenty years making clear: his work was centered on the spiritual evil to which some priests had fallen victim. His apostolate was not, as such, directed to the priest's physical, social or psychological disabilities, except as symptoms of the more radical sickness of soul.

The Pope went on. "Your work on their behalf," he compared, "is like that of the Good Samaritan, for you tend their wounds, nursing them back lovingly to spiritual health and clothing them again in the radiant vesture of sacerdotal fervor and grace." The comparison with the Good Samaritan of the Gospels was, in fact, one of Father Gerald's own favorite analogies for what he was doing for priests. Also, following Father Gerald almost verbatim, the Vicar of Christ emphasized that the priests were being tended in their wounds of spirit; that they were being nursed back to spiritual health, and that the evidence of their recovery would be to have them reclothed in God's supernatural grace and dedication to priestly piety.

Not satisfied with calling such priests "brother-pilgrims on the road of life," the Pope further declared that although "wounded in the fray, it is our duty to help them for they are our brothers, our sick brothers." Yet always the sickness of which the Pope speaks is neither physical nor emotional, but rather spiritual, in whose care the followers of Father Gerald were being so generously praised.

To further stress the spiritual nature of this sickness, the Holy Father explained what its symptoms in priests might be. "The Lord, once the cherished ideal of their lives, their loving companion in prayer, in preaching, in pastoral work for souls," had become less meaningful in their lives. Nevertheless, although they became estranged from Him, He did not abandon them. He is "still their Good Shepherd who will 'go after that which is lost until he finds it'" (Luke 15:4).

Such compassion on the part of Christ is only to be expected. For if He will do this "for even one of the hundred sheep, how much more will He seek out the shepherd himself should he stray in the mountain mists!" No one should be surprised at this. "Did He not do so for His first shepherd, Peter, who was moved to tears by His Master's loving gaze? Had He not the same forgiving gaze for His other apostle, Judas, as He addressed him by the sweet and intimate terms of 'friend'? But, alas, the traitor's heart was too hard for tears. And as with the lost sheep, so with the strayed shepherd, the Good Shepherd will even ease the fatigue of a long and sore-footed journey back to the fold, by 'laying him on his shoulders, rejoicing'" (Luke 15:5).

These memories from the Gospel are recalled by the Pope to remove any vestige of doubt that Father Gerald's work was, indeed, an apostolate. It was nothing less than the supernatural rehabilitation of priestly souls.

The Pontiff goes on to compare what the followers of the Good Shepherd were doing in the footsteps of Father Gerald. "Through your charity, and zeal," he told them, "the shattered fragments of the vessels of clay are pieced together again, and lovingly fashioned into their pristine beauty as 'vessels of election to carry Christ's name before the Gentiles'" (Acts 9:15). In context, the Savior was referring to St. Paul as His "vessel of election." Yet the Pope applied the title to all priests, as the Founder of the Paracletes so often had done in picturing the ideal priest as an imitator of the Apostle to the Gentiles. Strayed shepherds, the Pope would say, are like shattered vessels of clay that need to be put together again to serve as instruments of divine grace to other people.

Here Pope John touched on a cardinal premise of Father Gerald's methodology. Priests, he would say, fall from grace when they become discouraged. "Through your apostolate," the Pope was telling him, "the despairing receive spiritual health and vigor in living and life-giving identification with Christ the Eternal Priest." By saying this, the Pope was approving with pontifical sanction the mainstay of Father Gerald's mission to priests. What they need, and without which they spiritually die, is "identification with Christ the Eternal Priest." As they identify themselves by faith with the Master, and seek to further identify themselves by sacrifice, they not only recover from despair but become more vigorous than ever for having experienced the mercy of the Lord.

At this point, the Holy Father bears on the two principal means that Father Gerald insisted were indispensable to bring the shepherds back to the fold, namely the Eucharist and prayer.

> We read with particular pleasure, beloved son, that the central devotion in all houses of your Congregation is to our Eucharistic Lord. So, indeed, it should be. For the priest who has not the Blessed Sacrament in the center of his life cannot live his priesthood.

> We exhort you, likewise, to stress in our name the absolute necessity of fidelity to prayer in the sacerdotal life, for therein alone lies the unfailing means of ensuring the protection of the Power of God against all the powers of darkness.

The Eucharist and prayer! Pope John XXIII could not have been more emphatic, more explicit, or more absolute. A priest's life is either centered on the Blessed Sacrament or he has lost his direction as a priest and, the Pope would add, "cannot live his priesthood." This being said, it follows that to revitalize a man's priesthood, he must be brought back to a deep faith in the Real Presence and a strong devotion to the living Christ in the Eucharist.

Everything that Father Gerald stood for, and fought for, and was criticized for, was expressed by the Pope in this encomium on the Eucharist as pivotal to healing priests who are spiritually ill and restoring them to health as channels of divine grace to the people.

So, too, the Pontiff's insistence on prayer. He placed his finger on what Father Gerald in season and out of season kept saying was the single greatest cause of defection among the clergy and of unworthy priests in the Church: their neglect of prayer. Consequently, there is only one known remedy when they become supernaturally ill or diseased. They must return to the practice of what they had neglected, otherwise there is no cure for their malady. Why not? Because without prayer they will not obtain the grace they need to recuperate; since their basic trouble is not in the order of nature but in the order of grace. Only grace, to be gained by prayer, can cope with a problem which is beyond human solution. Here, if anywhere, it is literally true that what is impossible with man is possible with God, provided man has the humility to call upon God.

Not surprisingly, the Pope enjoins the practice of prayer among priests not only as an effective means of recovering spiritual health. He also promises those who pray the help from God to ward off the snares of the evil spirit, who is especially active in trying to seduce priests. Prayer, therefore, is both healing of the past and protective for the future.

Nothing was dearer to the heart of the Paraclete founder than to make sure that guest-priests who were restored to spiritual health would remain strong when they returned to the world. He was encouraged beyond words to have the Vicar of Christ tell him *in our name* to stress the *absolute necessity* of continued loyalty to prayer for priests to maintain themselves in the sacerdotal life.

THE PRACTICE OF FATHER GERALD

There is no simple way of either analyzing Father Gerald's method of dealing with the problems of priests or of classifying the means that he used. The reason is not because he was not systematic, since he could be very precise and organized, but because his approach was mainly spiritual and supernatural and therefore not easily reducible to familiar or even scientific terms.

At the masthead of his apostolate to priests was the name of the monastery he founded for their recovery, *Via Coeli,* the Way of Heaven. And so it was, the way or method that he followed and urged on those who would follow him, not the *via mundi,* the way of the world. Synonyms for his practice might be *Via Christi* (the Way of Christ) or *Via Fidei* (the Way of Faith), where the essential feature was whatever Christ and the Church taught was the best way to obtain or regain the rigorous life of grace that a priest needed to function properly as teacher of the faithful and dispenser of the mysteries of God.

Father Gerald assumed as beyond doubt that a priest's main purpose for existence, as a priest, was to lead people to heaven. If in the process of exercising his ministry, he had gone astray, or got "wounded in the fray," the only sensible thing is to find out what is wrong with him as a *priest* and treat his disordered condition accordingly. It would be unwise, to say the least, to treat him as just another individual and deal with his difficulties apart from that which by the sacrament of orders he really is. A priest is not simply another man, like everyone else. He is the anointed of the Lord and empowered to bring Christ Himself down to earth and enabled to reconcile sinners with an offended God. If he is in trouble, those who want to help him should not use only or even mainly such means as common sense indicates are useful for other people.

All the while, of course, Father Gerald recognized that a priest can get sick and physically or emotionally disabled like anyone else. But then he distinguished his apostolate from the humanitarian work of doctors or psychologists. By all means let physicians and therapists do what they can to assist priests on the purely human side of their disability; but concentrate in the apostolate on treating their souls, where the Spirit of God is active and where the healing powers of grace are to be sought through prayer and the sacraments instituted by Christ.

Love the Sinner. In dealing with priests who have gone astray, the first law of the apostolate in their favor is to love them. This is not easy. They can be "malevolent" and even "wicked." Yet if we wish to help them, "We must manifest towards them a great consideration. We must love them for what they could be, even if we cannot love them for what they are, for the possibility of good that resides in them."[1]

What makes this difficult is not only the natural reluctance to show affection for selfish and unaffectionate people. It is also the problem of carefully distinguishing the sinner from his sin. The love that needs to be shown must be carefully balanced. "In our sympathy for the sinner," we must also "get across to the individual sinner our horror of sin. We must not minimize sin, that is not true pity," and it is not true love.

> If a man, above all a Priest of God, has not a horror of sin, he is in danger of hell fire. Let us pray for the grace that is so precious, especially to a priest, a horror of even venial sin. Therefore, while we must have a constant sympathy for the casualties of God's officers, yet we must not fail to ask God that in our ready sympathy for the casualties we should aid them in such a way as to help God to bring home to the soul the salvific sense they can be forgiven as

was Peter when he *realized* that he had denied the Son of God.

Let me illustrate what I mean, and if you feel that you cannot accept it, then find another place to serve God, for you cannot help the apostolate which God has placed on my shoulders. Peter denied the Master and went out weeping. Suppose John had gone and minimized the offense. Undoubtedly John did go to him and say something like this: "Go back, Peter, He has forgiven you, I know!" but he *didn't* say: "It doesn't matter — everybody does it!" It is Catholic philosophy that the whole world may better perish than one mortal sin be committed, and Jesus Christ taught us that the greatest sin is the sin of scandal: "If any man gives scandal to one of these little ones, it were better for him not to have been born."[2]

What the founder of the Paracletes was saying is that in dealing with priests who have compromised, the love shown them must be genuine and self-sacrificing. But it must be a love based on the truth. Sin is sin and no amount of sympathy for the sinner should obscure the fact that losing the state of grace is the worst evil in the world.

In order to motivate his men to show a compassion for stray shepherds, Father Gerald encouraged them to meditate on the compassionate Sorrowful Mother and reflect on "how tenderly the Mother of God bends over the souls of Christians who are in mortal sin." The Pieta, after all, represents not only the scene on Calvary when the dead Christ was taken down from the Cross but the situation today whenever a Christian, and especially a priest, is estranged from God. "So our Blessed Mother, the mother of all mothers, bends over the souls in the Church that are the living image of her dead Son, and works and labors and prays unceasingly, making with her Divine Son unceasing representation before the throne of God, that her first-born Son might not have died in vain for these other Christs."[3]

This is the model of loving kindness that "these other Christs" should be shown, no matter how badly they have injured the Christ who ordained them.

Overcome Discouragement. Experience shows that for those who have deeply sinned and find themselves steeped in some vice, the hardest thing to do is cope with discouragement. There is an inner monitor that tells such people they have done wrong and, as in the case of priests, they often detest themselves to the point of despair. The case of Judas is a sad example for all times. They must therefore be reminded of God's loving forgiveness.

Speaking to the Paracletes, Father Gerald told them they have the unique privilege "of extending the invitation of love to those who have betrayed Our Lord."

> Our vocation is equivalent as if Our Lord had said to John or Peter: Judas is in despair. Go tell him that my Heart is still waiting for him. Give him the message of my love. Tell him he has already acknowledged his sin. All he needs to do now is to say: My Jesus forgives me. That is our work that Christ has given us to do, to bring the unfathomable riches of His Divine mercy to the attention of shepherds who have failed and who are potentially the objects of the fertile ground for the seeds of despair.[4]

It is impossible to exaggerate the value of this approach. Yet to continue doing it day after day will require above ordinary strength and motivation. Hence the need to call on supernatural reserves.

> Pray for that most valuable grace for the Paraclete specifically in his vocation that when you see a Priest despondent, beaten down, you will see in him Jesus Christ and that you will be constrained by the Holy Spirit, by the charity of God to go to help him. By encouragement, by a smile, by a little conversation, by watching, if necessary, by his bedside, whatever he requires, give it to him, in *nomine Domini*. Let us step up to a priest quietly and without ostentation but effectively, even as St. Camillus de Lellis bent over his poor wretched fever victims and whispered: "Lord Jesus, what can I do for you?"

> Bend over these priests, humbly, eagerly, patiently and lift the cross. Try to lift it at least. The figure is very perfect because Simon of Cyrene only helped Our Lord to

carry the Cross; he didn't carry it entirely. He helped Our Lord to carry it, and all we can do for any of our fellow beings, is help them. A priest is another Christ. These priests are going by, weak, at times beaten down. They have to be helped. We can't take the cross away from them but we can help them carry it.[5]

To keep this inspiration alive in their minds, Father Gerald gave the Paracletes the following as a "guiding principle or maxim: Every priest is my brother. Let us deal as patiently, as tenderly, as consistently in perseverance with a priest as if he were our own brother. After all every priest is our brother because we are of the Blood of Jesus Christ. We have been dominated by the infusion of the Precious Blood."[6]

Even naturally, people respond to kindness; but since the discouragement of priests is deeper than mere nature, it takes grace to help them conquer their despondency. This grace can be merited by the prayer and gentle patience of those who take care of them.

Father Gerald confessed that he had to pray "for the grace to be patient with those who fall over and over again." In order to motivate himself, he would argue this way: "God has been reasonable with me in my own unreasonableness. Shall I not therefore be patient with my fellow creature, and I shall do it to repay God for His patience with me."[7]

What is often most trying in working with priests in trouble is their inveterate tendency to discouragement. "This is one of the heaviest hidden crosses here at Via Coeli." Christ knew that the vast majority of mankind would have to lift themselves up over and over again from physical weakness, from spiritual weakness. It is hard to begin again. It is hard for men. There is a terrible downdraft that brings discouragement upon the soul. What's the use. I fail, I have failed. I can't go on through this all again. "All of this the Savior foresaw, the terrible temptations not to rise again." That is why "Our dear Lord, with the generous complete dedication of Himself to teach us in every way, to show us how to redeem ourselves, permitted Himself to sink down exhausted" once, twice and three times under the Cross, "and then to get up and go on."[8]

Those who deal with priests must themselves be thus highly inspired, so they can pass on the inspiration to those whose faith alone will enable them, perhaps in spite of repeated failures "to get up and go on."

Restore Union with God. In all this effort at rehabilitation one point must be kept in mind, and it is crucial to the whole apostolate. Since the basic problem with priests who defect or go astray is failure in the interior life, this must be restored at all costs.

> By way of prelude, a priest should become convinced that he has been specially, indeed distinctively called by God. He has invited us from among all the thousands of mankind. He has called upon priests to help Him in the salvation of our fellow men. O Lord what a privilege. Thou who art God hast invited me, a little creature, to come and help You to save the world. Why? That is veiled in the mysterious depths of Thy predilection and of Thy love, for when God calls a man to a special service, He does so out of love.[9]

How is it that men who have been thus dearly loved should ever turn their backs on the Lord who called them and "give up" their priesthood for a mess of pottage? The reason is not so much a reason as a fact of sacred history. They let go of the interior life. Already in the Old Testament, Yahweh said to one of the patriarchs, "Walk before me and be perfect."

> God says to His priests in the greater intimacy of the New Testament: the greater intimacy between God and man that had its source in the Infinite Love of God and was activated in the Incarnation. Not "walk before me" but "O my priests, walk with me, nay live in me and let me live in you."

> One of the great sources, one of the great occasions for the defection of priests is in their infidelities, from their infidelities to Christ and the Church, it is that they have failed to attain to this interior union with God at least as an abiding, habitual grace. They have no interior life, and therefore, the interior faculties of their soul, their intellect

and will and memory, do not find in Christ the great consolation that awaits the soul that cultivates an interior life.[10]

Here we touch on one of the unique features of the apostolate
to priests. Like everyone else, a priest must find satisfaction in his
way of life. He must enjoy dealing with souls, and preaching to the
people, and catechizing children, and offering Mass, and attending
the sick, and counseling the faithful, and administering the sacraments. Naturally he will find his life burdensome and many of the
demands of his priestly vocation exacting. Human nature can become oppressed, or bored, or simply fatigued with the effort and rou-
tine. Add to this the simple fact that a priest is vowed to celibacy, and
to strive after sanctity, and it is not surprising that he needs to be
sustained from within if he wants to persevere in his priesthood and
even grow in his chosen calling.

Father Gerald keeps coming back to this truth with a frequency
that might seem excessive, except that he realized as few others how
fundamental it is to any lasting apostolate among priests. What exactly does he mean? He means that just as the basic need in a priest's
life is to give himself entirely to God, so the only effective way of
converting him — if he has fallen into habits of sin — is through the
patient ministry of other priests whose lives are an inspiration for
him to follow.

Thus every problem in a priest's life can be reduced to this:
"After having accepted God's choice by entering into the obligations
of the priesthood," he then chooses "something else in preference to
God. Therefore our basic and psychological problem is to persuade
priests to come back to their first choice; to choose God and God
alone, to choose God supremely by a sovereign love, like St. Thomas
Aquinas," who when asked, "What dost thou ask?", answered, "Only
thyself, Lord."[11]

Given the weakness of human nature, however, priests will
scarcely make this kind of re-dedication unless they see others, especially other priests, "quite evidently choosing God" themselves. It is
hard enough to make the self-consecration in the first place; it is
superhumanly difficult to recover the generosity after this has been
culpably lost. In the ordinary course of Providence, the inspiration to

do so must come from the outside. This explains Father Gerald's plea for holiness among those who undertake to re-sanctify the Church's priests.

> Unless it is obvious to our priest-guests that we as individuals and as a Community are quite evidently choosing God then we shall have a very difficult time persuading them to choose God. It would be so easy for the devil or for their own souls to reflect: Well they say to choose God but they haven't done it themselves.

> We must be ourselves sold on God. We must be sold on Christ with all our heart and mind and whole being. That is the great reason why the Church is not sweeping in our day and in any day, everything before it. We have the Teacher. We have the living Christ. We have Christ in His humanity. We have His sacraments. We have His authority. They have rowed away from the Bark of Peter expecting it to sink but somehow it never sinks. "The gates of hell shall not prevail against her." She isn't going to sink.

> Why is it we do not persuade more to come back aboard this sea-worthy vessel that will wrestle with the winds and the sea until it is brought by the Divine pilot into the port of eternal rest? There is so much waiting for us.[12]

What is the answer? The answer in the world at large and in working with priests is that those engaged in the apostolate are not holy enough. "If we can only be saints, nothing can stop us." And more pertinently, "When Christ is supreme in the soul of a priest, nothing can stop him."[13] If he labors among priests to bring them back to Christ, they will return — provided they see his laboring with an "overwhelming love of God," and see him "deliberately trample on" anything that challenges "the supremacy of this love."[14]

Have Them Pray. The role of prayer in the restoration of priests to sacerdotal fidelity comes in two stages, where each stage complements the other. There must be prayer, much prayer, joined with sacrifice, by others than the priest. They must invoke God's mercy to open the mind and heart of a priest and bring him to his senses. It may be called the prayer of conversion.

But once a priest has been so far touched by grace, he must start praying himself. Otherwise the gift of seeing the light and recognizing his need of God will go wasted, as Father Gerald admitted happened at Via Coeli. "We have every evidence," he said, "that a priest who was saying Mass was at the same time plotting the betrayal of the Master. He had no intention of permanent reform." Rather he "was using his retreat here and the magnificent opportunity of conversion merely as a cover for further liberty in the exercise of his own particular passion."[15] There may have been the original grace from God to break with his life of sin, and this brought him to Via Coeli. But there was no follow up; the priest did not carry through, and the result was disastrous.

The Paraclete founder was fond of comparing the apostolate of priests to what happened to Saul on his way to Damascus. "Every priest," he thought, "who comes to us with the proper motivation has been struck down on the road to Damascus. Bent upon persecuting Christ, Christ has reached down and in one way or another Divine Providence has brought him to his knees"[6].

So far, the totally undeserved grace merited by others may seem to have been active. But this is only the beginning. "Then a man must be led; he cannot help himself. The sinner cannot help himself." No doubt "the grace of conversion is a true grace," but it needs to be assisted from the outside, that is, by another or other human beings. And this is the indispensable role of those whom Father Gerald was forming into apostles of the priesthood.

> Our beautiful vocation is like that of the attendants of St. Paul who led him into Damascus. He was blind. They led him to the city of Hope. They led him to the city where he was to meet Christ, where he was to receive Christ, where he was to receive his eyesight. And if a man makes use of his retreat in one of our monasteries properly, then he, too, will presently receive his sight. The scales of false values will fall from his eyes. He will see clearly as he never saw before the way he must go with Christ and one of you will bear the part of Ananias who will come and say: Saul, the Lord Jesus has sent me to you to show you how much you are a vessel of election by the very fact

that you are a priest. And He will show you how much you must suffer for His name's sake[7].

Then comes the responsibility of the priest himself. Once Saul had been struck down, miraculously, by God's grace, he did what every converted sinner must immediately do, at the risk of losing the fruits of his conversion. He, personally, on his own, must pray.

What did Our Lord say to Ananias? He said to Ananias: "Behold he prayeth." One of the things that we must emphasize by word and example in the life of our retreatants, is the value of prayer. Without prayer there can be no salvation. God requires that cry from the human heart. He inspires it but even when He inspires it not everyone is ready to correspond.

The moral to be learned from this revealed event in the life of St. Paul is clear. Those who labor for priests "must ceaselessly invoke the Holy Spirit of God to give the grace of prayer" to those who have been initially converted from sin; which really means to ask for the grace that will move the converted man to pray. "There is the secret. The man who prays and who perseveres in prayer will doubtlessly come to salvation. God recognizes the basic good will that underlies all good prayer."[18]

To repeat Father Gerald, "There is the secret." Any sinner who in pride or lust turns away from God does not, of himself, have the strength even to turn to God and much less return to Him with all his heart. Such a person needs actual grace from the Lord whom he has rejected.

If by divine mercy he is inspired, like Saul, to want to reform, this is only because of God's condescension. It is also only the beginning. Ahead of him lies the prospect of giving up his former ways, of sacrificing the praise and adulation he may have been getting from those who approve his manner of life, of letting go of such money or friends or prestige as living by the standards of the world often brings, of breaking bad habits that may be binding him like chains and that he shudders to think what effort this will take; of withdrawing from creatures to which he has become addicted, and he foresees the agony of the withdrawal pains. All of this and more the sinner has to face, as the price of his reformation. It is the inevitable sanction for break-ing God's commandments, and can no more be avoided than the con-sequences of ignoring the laws of gravity.

There is no way a person in this situation can make it alone. He needs help from other people, and extraordinary help from God. The best help that others can give him is to urge him to pray. If he prays, but only if he does, divine grace will not be wanting and the reforma-tion already begun will take root and grow, as it did in Saul of Tarsus, until it reaches even sanctity.

Faith tells us that God never demands the impossible. This does not mean, however, that we may not find ourselves in circumstances where it is humanly impossible to do what needs to be done, as in the case of sinners who want to reform. At this point of crisis, if the sinner prays, he will obtain the light and strength from on high that he lacks from below and the return to God becomes not only possible but even easy; certainly easier than a person's fearful imagination would suggest.

If the one who contemplates returning to God is a priest, prayer is, if anything, more necessary. Why? Because as one who knows better, his guilt is greater; and because often there are more human ties that bind a priest's estrangement to the practice of virtue. Add to this what Father Gerald never tired repeating, that the evil spirit is most active in seducing priests, so that the need for prayer, earnest, deep and humble prayer by a priest for himself becomes absolutely imperative.

Resources to the Eucharist. But not just any form of prayer is to be practiced by those who wish to follow through on their initial grace of conversion. Especially for priests, it should be prayer to the Holy Eucharist.

That is why Father Gerald liked to hear the Jemez Canyon called "Canyon of the Blessed Sacrament." As we have seen at length, in Father Gerald's mind, devotion to the Blessed Sacrament is of the essence of priestly piety. It is certainly of the essence of priestly ref-ormation. For if neglect of the Eucharist is the main single cause of infidelity among priests, then devotion to Christ in the Eucharist is correspondingly necessary for restoring them to the faithful service of God. Reserving the Blessed Sacrament and making its Presence available everywhere and at any time of the day or night was part of Father Gerald's master plan for priests. It is also the part of Father Gerald's methodology that Pope John read about "with particular pleasure." It was in praising this practice that the Holy Father made the astounding but very true statement that "the priest who has not the Blessed Sacrament in the center of his life cannot live the priesthood." To which we might now add, nor can a priest recover his priesthood except by the same Eucharistic means. It becomes less surprising then for the Paraclete founder to say what he did about the basic pedagogy that priests in trouble have to be taught.

> What we are trying to do here is to teach priests to realize what it means to live under the same roof with the Son of God. Here is the answer to all problems: material, physical, spiritual. Here is a God who loves us and counts our heartbeats, which is something that we would grow tired of doing. But the Son of God never grows tired of keeping and counting the heartbeats of men, and especially the heartbeats of His priests. They are His own heartbeats! They are (if that would be possible) affectively, it would seem, dearer to Him than His own heartbeats, for His heartbeat stopped on the Cross that our heartbeats might be rhythmed with His for all eternity, that we might not lose life everlasting. Here is the answer to all problems.[19]

This is saying a lot, and apart from faith it may seem to be saying too much. What, someone may object, the Presence of the Eucharist is *the* answer to all problems? How unrealistic can you be?

But Father Gerald was so convinced of this fact that he staked his whole apostolate on fidelity to the practice of adoration before the Blessed Sacrament. He saw in the Eucharist what faith tells every believer, that the Son of God who became the Son of Mary, is really, truly and bodily present in the Sacrament of the altar. Since it is the same Jesus who worked miracles in Palestine, why should He not continue working miracles now, especially for His priests. "Here is the God all love, for all problems find their solution in that Supreme Love," who became man and, not merely dwelt, but *dwells* among us.[20] And "from His fullness we have, all of us, received" (John 1:16), but only in the measure of our faith. To rekindle this faith in priests is the surest way of restoring them to loyalty in their ministry.

Along with devotion to the Real Presence, the offering of Mass by a priest is a powerful source of grace. In the early years of Via Coeli, guest-priests were not given the privilege of saying Mass unless, or until, they were fully rehabilitated and, in fact, canonically reinstated with the Church. One of Father Gerald's long-cherished hopes was to obtain a mitigation of this severe, though understandable, rule. Finally he appealed personally to the Roman Pontiff, then Pope Pius XII. His account of what happened in Rome is revealing. "As regards the Mass for our longtime retreatants," he said, referring to the priests-on-probation, "the Holy Father himself said to me in private audience last Thursday when I had explained my conviction that the Mass should be considered not as a privilege but as the Daily Bread of these penitents — he himself replied at once, 'for their spiritual life.' this is a direct quote and expresses the whole attitude of our saintly Holy Father."[21]

As with the Real Presence, so with the Mass, Father Gerald recognized the Eucharist as a phenomenal source of grace. That is why he did not hesitate to say of Via Coeli, "we must aspire to make this mountain canyon another Lourdes. Our particular apostolate is to cure the afflicted among God's Shepherds."[22] But this was also the Canyon of the Blessed Sacrament.

Whatever else a priest in trouble needs it is the conviction that "The answer to our priestly needs, the secret of priestly happiness, the source of priestly zeal and contentment, the love our hearts, like all other hearts, craves by their very nature — all these things are to be found in the cultivation of a personal devotion to our Divine Lover in the Sacrament of His Love."[23] To recover one's faith in this truth is the essence of Father Gerald's method of reclaiming strayed shepherds. Everything else, as important as it may be, is secondary. This stands to reason, since only God can work miracles, and the Incarnate God is present and active on earth in the Holy Eucharist.

BIOGRAPHICAL SKETCH

OCTOBER 29, 1894
Second child born to Michael Edward Fitzgerald and Mary Elizabeth Brassil in South Framingham, Massachusetts.

NOVEMBER 4, 1894
Baptized at St. George Church in Saxonville, Massachusetts. Baptismal name, Gerald Cushing Fitzgerald.

1912
Graduated from Weymouth High School, president of his class, editor of the school paper "The Nineteen Twelve".

SEPTEMBER 16, 1912
Entered Boston College, became associate editor of college paper "The Stylus" in his junior, senior years.

JUNE 15, 1916
Graduated from Boston College.

AUTUMN OF 1916
Entered St. John's Seminary in Brighton, Mass.

MAY 26, 1921, Feast of Corpus Christi
Ordained at Cathedral of Holy Cross in Boston. Richard J. Cushing was in the same class and graduated the same day; he went on to become Archbishop and then Cardinal of Boston.

MAY 29, 1921
First solemn Mass at St. Peter's Church in Cambridge.

JUNE 8, 1921 TO SEPTEMBER 6, 1921
First assignment as curate at St. Margaret in Brockton, Mass.

SEPTEMBER 6, 1921, TO NOVEMBER 7, 1933
Second assignment as curate at Our Lady of the Presentation, Brighton district of Boston; started "Letters of the late Father Page."

NOVEMBER 21, 1933, Feast of Our Lady of the Presentation
Entered the novitiate of the Congregation of Holy Cross — St. Joseph in Ste. Genevieve near Montreal, Quebec. His novitiate began December 3, 1933.

DECEMBER 8, 1934
Profession of first vows under the name of Rev. Michael Joseph Cushing Fitzgerald, C.S.C. Psalm 121:1 chosen for profession announcement.

1935
First assignment as assistant to the Rector of Holy Cross Seminary in North Easton, Mass. Taught English and Religion; began as preacher of novenas and giving retreats.

AUTUMN OF 1936
Appointed Rector of Holy Cross Seminary and remained until December of 1942.

DECEMBER 1942
Volunteered as Military Chaplain (Army) at 48 years of age.

FEBRUARY 1943
Attended Chaplains' School at Harvard University, returned to New York City as Secretary at the Military Ordinate on Madison Avenue; Archbishop Francis J. Spellman, Military Vicar of the Armed Forces of the U.S., was in charge of this office.

1943
Elected to the Gallery of Catholic Authors. Became known as the "soldier-poet."

APRIL 1945
His father, Michael Edward, died unaware his son was overseas in Manila.

SUMMER 1945
Wrote from Manila to Archbishop Cushing of Boston and Archbishop Spellman of New York about an apostolate to assist military chap-

lains and priests who were ill or aged, especially spiritual help to revitalize their vocations and help restore them to their priestly ministry.

AUGUST 30, 1945
Archbishop Cushing of Boston wrote Father Gerald that a suitable place in Gloucester, Mass., had been found and the Brothers of St. John of God would operate it until Father arrived.

SEPTEMBER 1945
Archbishop Spellman came to Manila; Father Gerald explained his proposed apostolate for priests. The Archbishop invited him to establish the work in his archdiocese.

DECEMBER 8, 1945
De-activated from service at Fort Devins, Mass., assigned to Holy Cross Mission Band in North Easton.

1946
Traveled extensively looking for a suitable place to begin the work for priests.

NOVEMBER 30, 1946
Received a reply from Archbishop Edwin V. Byrne to start his communities: Servants of the Holy Paraclete, a community of priests and brothers; Handmaids of the Precious Blood, a community of sisters in the Archdiocese of Santa Fe, New Mexico.

FIRST WEEK IN DECEMBER 1946
Flew to New Mexico. Received a warm welcome from Archbishop Byrne who had Father taken to view two properties. He chose the vacated Mountain Inn in Jemez Springs, located near the 17th century ruins of a Franciscan Mission.

DECEMBER 26, 1946
Left Holy Cross Seminary in North Easton with friends and drove to New Mexico.

JANUARY 4, 1947
Arrived in Jemez Springs.

JANUARY 5, 1947
Feast of the Holy Name of Jesus. Father offered the Sacrifice of the

Mass at the Mountain Inn which Father named "Via Coeli." The Servants of the Paraclete were inaugurated.

FEBRUARY 4, 1947
Father wrote: "Now we're three priests — will probably have eight priests before the month ends."

MAY 22, 1947
Three candidates arrived from the East for the Handmaids of the Precious Blood. Their first convent was a small rented house. They began to wear blue uniforms.

MAY 25, 1947, Pentecost Sunday
Foundation Day of the Handmaids of the Precious Blood. Father Gerald offered Mass in their convent for five aspirants, and appointed as Superior Mother Ancilla.

JUNE 11, 1947
Received a letter from the Apostolic Delegate congratulating him on the two new communities.

JULY 1, 1947
Archbishop Byrne conducted investiture ceremonies for both communities.

EARLY AUGUST 1947
Rapid growth of both communities: twenty-six priests, three brothers, and more coming. "Twelve Handmaid aspirants."

SEPTEMBER 12, 1947
Sent two rules to Rome with a request that two novitiates be sanctioned.

APRIL 1948
Archbishop Byrne conducted an investiture ceremony for two brothers and five priests. Fr. Gerald now exchanged his black Holy Cross Habit for the gray of the Servants of the Paraclete and took the name, Gerald of the Holy Spirit, s.P. Also a medical clinic was opened named Villa Cor Jesu.

MAY 1948
First ordination to the priesthood of the Servants of the Paraclete in the cathedral in Santa Fe.

OCTOBER 1948
Ground broken for new chapel for the priests.

JANUARY 4, 1949
Telephone call from Archbishop Byrne with the first approval of the two rules from Rome.

MARCH 25, 1950
Mother M. Dolorosa was appointed Superior of the Handmaids.

APRIL, 1950
The Sponsor, a leaflet, was first published.

OCTOBER 1950
Archbishop Byrne asked the Handmaids to staff the Villa Therese Medical Clinic for the Poor in Santa Fe; they continued until August 1981 when the Sisters of Charity replaced them.

1951
The Servants of the Paraclete sheltered over 200 priests during the last four years.

JUNE 1, 1952, Pentecost
The Servants of the Paraclete were canonically erected as a Congregation of diocesan right by Archbishop Byrne.

JUNE 7, 1952
Father Gerald flew to Rome and was received in private audience by Pope Pius XII.

JUNE 20, 1952, Feast of the Sacred Heart
Father Gerald made profession of perpetual vows.

JULY 5, 1952
Archbishop Byrne offered Mass at Via Coeli and appointed Father Gerald the Superior General of the community.

1953
Father Gerald had his second audience with Pope Pius XII.

AUGUST 22, 1956
The Handmaids of the Precious Blood were canonically erected as a Congregation of diocesan right by Archbishop Byrne. He appointed Mother M. Dolorosa as first Superior General.

1956
488 priests have been sheltered in the care of the Servants of the Paraclete.

1957
The Sponsor became a magazine with a monthly circulation of 10,000.

MAY 17, 1958
Fr. Gerald's mother, Mary Elizabeth Brassil Fitzgerald, died.

1958
A new chapel and novitiate were built for the Handmaids.

1959
Pope John XXIII received Father Gerald and followed their visit with a letter of commendation.

1961
A house for the Servants of the Paraclete was established in Rome and for a period of time was called the Generalate; and another house in Montopoli, Italy was opened.

1962
The Shrine Church of Mary, Mother of Priests was built in Jemez Springs near Via Coeli.

1963, 1965
Father Gerald was received in private audience by Pope Paul VI.

1965
The Servants of the Paraclete opened a home in England, two houses in South America, one in Africa, and new houses in the United States. The Handmaids opened a convent in Vermont.

JANUARY 1, 1966
Father Gerald opened the "Queen of Peace" for priests in Dumfriesshire, Scotland.

1967
Father Gerald established the Maison du Divin Paraclit in Jallais, France, which is owned and financed by the bishops.

1968
The Handmaids assumed responsibility for The Sponsor. Villa Louis Martin (Infirmary), Jemez Springs, NM, was built by the Servants of the Paraclete with financial help from the Bishops of the United States.

MAY 21, 1969
Father Gerald's 48th anniversary of his ordination.

JUNE 28, 1969, 6:00 P.M.
Father Gerald died in Marlboro, Massachusetts, giving a retreat for lay teachers.

JULY 4TH, 1969
Father Gerald was buried in Resurrection Cemetery of the Servants of the Paraclete, Jemez Springs, New Mexico, with military honors.

REFERENCES

INTRODUCTION
[1] Homily in the Vatican Basilica, June 29, 1978
[2] Letter to all priests, Holy Thursday, 1979

I. MODERN SECULARISM AND THE PRIESTHOOD
[1] Conference to Servants of the Paraclete, April 28, 1955
[2] Conference to Handmaids of the Precious Blood, May 1968
[3] Ibid.
[4] Ibid.
[5] Ibid.
[6] Ibid., March 28, 1949
[7] Conference to Servants of the Paraclete, August 1956
[8] Ibid., August 5, 1956
[9] Ibid., January 1, 1955
[10] Ibid.
[11] Ibid.
[12] Ibid., September 1, 1955
[13] Ibid.
[14] Ibid., December 17, 1955
[15] Conference to Handmaids of the Precious Blood, February 1969
[16] Ibid.
[17] Ibid.
[18] Conference to Parish Visitors of Mary Immaculate, June 1942
[19] Ibid.
[20] Conference to Servants of the Paraclete, September 9, 1954
[21] Ibid., September 1956
[22] Ibid.

II. What Is a Priest?
[1] Conference to Handmaids of the Precious Blood, December 16, 1959

III. The Virtues of a Priest
[1] Conference to Servants of the Paraclete, February 24, 1969
[2] Ibid.
[3] Ibid.
[4] Ibid., December 20, 1954
[5] Ibid., January 15, 1955
[6] Ibid., December 20, 1954
[7] Ibid.
[8] Ibid.
[9] Ibid.
[10] Ibid., April 28, 1955
[11] Ibid., June 26, 1954
[12] Ibid.
[13] Ibid., April 28, 1955
[14] Ibid.
[15] Ibid.
[16] Ibid.
[17] Ibid., February 17, 1969
[18] Ibid., August 24, 1954
[19] Ibid., June 26, 1954
[20] Ibid., August 1956
[21] Ibid.
[22] Ibid.
[23] Ibid.
[24] Ibid., April 28, 1955
[25] Ibid., September 4, 1954
[26] Ibid., January 25, 1955
[27] Ibid.
[28] Ibid.

IV. We Can Achieve What We Will
[1] Ibid., February 24, 1969
[2] Ibid.
[3] Ibid.
[4] Ibid.

[5] Ibid., May 21, 1954

[6] Ibid.

[7] Ibid.

V. The Humanity of Christ

[1] Ibid., May 19, 1954

[2] The Path of Love, 61, Fr. G. Fitzgerald, Fredrick Pustet Co., 1943

[3] Ibid.

[4] Conference to Handmaids of the Precious Blood, June 3, 1954

[5] Ibid.

[6] Ibid.

[7] Ibid.

[8] Ibid.

[9] Ibid.

[10] Ibid.

[11] Ibid.

[12] Ibid.

[13] Ibid.

[14] *Redemptor Hominis,* 20

[15] Conference to Handmaids of the Precious Blood, April 21, 1969

[16] Ibid.

[17] Ibid.

[18] Ibid.

VI. Relationship to Christ

[1] Conference to Servants of the Paraclete, January 19, 1955

[2] Ibid.

[3] Ibid.

[4] Ibid.

[5] *Sponsor*, July 1950

[6] Letters of Father Page, 178-179, Longmans Green, New York, 1940

[7] Ibid., 169-170

[8] Ibid., 159-160

[9] Ibid., 161-162

[10] Conference to Handmaids of the Precious Blood, June 1950

[11] Conference to Servants of the Paraclete, January 16, 1955

[12] Ibid.

[13] Ibid.

[14] Address of Pope John Paul II to the American Bishops, Chicago, October 5, 1979

[15] Conference to Servants of the Paraclete, January 16, 1955

[16] Ibid.

[17] Ibid.

[18] Ibid.

[19] Ibid.

[20] Ibid., May 19, 1954

[21] Ibid.

[22] Ibid.

[23] Ibid.

VII. LIVING THE MASS

[1] Ibid.

[2] Ibid.

[3] Ibid.

[4] Ibid.

[5] Ibid.

[6] Ibid.

[7] Ibid.

[8] Ibid.

[9] Ibid., September 14, 1954

[10] Ibid.

VIII. THE PRIEST AND MARY

[1] Ibid., September 18, 1954

[2] Ibid.

[3] Ibid.

[4] Ibid.

[5] Ibid., September 4, 1954

[6] Ibid., September 9, 1954

[7] Ibid.

[8] Conference to Handmaids of the Precious Blood, 1950

[9] Conference to Servants of the Paraclete, September 4, 1954

[10] Ibid.

[11] Ibid.

[12] Ibid.

[13] Ibid.

[14] *Sponsor*, October 1950, pg. 1

[15] Ibid., pg. 2

[16] Conference to Servants of the Paraclete, September 9, 1954

[17] Ibid.

[18] Address at the Shrine of Our Lady of Knock, September 30, 1979

[19] Conference to Servants of the Paraclete, September 11, 1954

[20] Ibid., September 18, 1954

[21] Ibid., February 1, 1969

[22] Ibid.

[23] Ibid., September 11, 1954

[24] Ibid., January 28, 1955

[25] Ibid., September 11, 1954

[26] Ibid.

[27] Ibid., June 26, 1954

[28] Ibid.

[29] Conference to Handmaids of the Precious Blood, 1950

IX. THE HOLY HOUR

[1] Paraclete Customs, 10

[2] Conference to Servants of the Paraclete, August 24, 1954

[3] Ibid.

[4] Ibid., August 26, 1954

[5] Ibid.

[6] Ibid.

[7] Ibid.

[8] Ibid.

[9] Ibid.

[10] Ibid.

[11] Ibid.

[12] Ibid.

[13] Ibid.

X. PRIESTLY CELIBACY

[1] Conference to Handmaids of the Precious Blood, June 1950

[2] Conference to Servants of the Paraclete, December 25, 1954

[3] Ibid., May 5, 1954

[4] Ibid., September 16, 1954

[5] Ibid.

[6] Ibid., December 25, 1954

[7] Ibid.

[8] Conference to Handmaids of the Precious Blood, 1950

[9] Conference to Servants of the Paraclete, December 25, 1954

[10] A Holy Hour for Seminarians

[11] Conference to Servants of the Paraclete, August 1956

[12] Ibid.

[13] Ibid.

[14] Ibid.

[15] Ibid.

XI. PRAYING FOR PRIESTS

[1] Homily of Pope John Paul II, October 17, 1978

[2] Conference to Handmaids of the Precious Blood

[3] Ibid.

[4] Ibid.

[5] Retreat to Parish Visitors of Mary Immaculate, June 28, 1942

[6] Ibid.

[7] Letters of Father Page

[8] Ibid.

[9] Conference to Servants of the Paraclete, June 23, 1954

[10] Conference to Handmaids of the Precious Blood

[11] Conference to Servants of the Paraclete, June 23, 1954

[12] Ibid.

[13] Ibid.

[14] Ibid.

[15] Ibid., August 26, 1954

XII. Caring for Priests

[1] Ibid., September 4, 1954

[2] Conference to Handmaids of the Precious Blood, August 15, 1950

[3] Conference to Servants of the Paraclete, September 18, 1954

[4] Ibid., February 24, 1969

[5] Ibid., January 28, 1955

[6] Ibid., January 29, 1955

[7] Ibid.

[8] Ibid.

[9] Ibid., February 24, 1969

[10] Ibid, August 24, 1954

[11] Ibid., February 24, 1969

[12] Ibid.

[13] Ibid.

[14] Ibid.

[15] Ibid., January 13, 1955

[16] Ibid., January 25, 1955

[17] Ibid.

[18] Ibid.

[19] Ibid., July 7, 1958

[20] Ibid.

[21] Letter to Mother Dolorosa, December 21, 1953

[22] Conference to Handmaids of the Precious Blood, 1949

[23] Letters of Father Page, 193

Subject Index

Adoration (see also Blessed Sacrament)
    imitation of Christ's, 11-12
    method of aspirations, 12
    of Blessed Sacrament, 98-100
    of creatures, inordinate, 108

Affluence
    indifference to other's needs developed by, 9
    money becomes the guiding motive, 1-2
    self-centeredness promoted by, 8

Apostolate
    union with God necessary for effectiveness of, 14-16

Atheism
    emptiness of, 9

Blessed Sacrament (see Eucharist and Real Presence)
    All Love, loving, 58, 141-142
    Christ adored, 98-100, 140-142
    devotion to, 54-58, 97, 129, 140-141
    prayer before, 103, 107-108
    reason for title of, 52, 57-58
    relation to vocations, 31, 56
    sanctifies those receiving, 52, 114
    tenderness of God in, 57
    unchanging love of, 56, 57, 107

Blessed Virgin (see also Mary and Sorrowful Mother)
    fruitful in virginity, 70
    priests' devotion to, 24, 85-96, 109-110
    spiritual motherhood of, 85-86, 92

Holiness

impossible without grace, 89

inspires others, 14-15, 136

necessary in the apostolate, 137

Holy Hour

daily recommended, 97-98

graces won through, 104

method for, 98-104

results of, 97-98

Holy Spirit

convicts world of sin, 73

fills priests' souls with love of Mary, 90

invoked for grace of prayer, 139

Human will (see Free will)

blessing of a good will, 48-49

desire to expiate and, 122

immolation to Divine Will, 62

liberty of, 43, 45

needs strengthening by self-denial and prayer, 46-48

only free when following God's will, 46-48

pray for a strong will, 48

reduced by psychological and social sciences, 45

weakened by sin, 46

Humanity of Christ

hypostatic union, 51-54

indispensable way to intimacy with God, 53

plenitude of grace from, 54

Humility

before our fellowman, 33-34

born of faith, 10

brings peace of heart, 33

cultivate by prayer, 34-35

example of Christ's, 32, 34-35

form of charity, 34

necessary for intimacy with Christ, 32

necessary in the life of a priest, 32, 129

worldliness overcome by, 10